Listen!
Our Dying
Saviour
Speaks

Listen! Our Dying Saviour Speaks

Lehman Strauss

LOIZEAUX BROTHERS

Neptune, New Jersey

First Printing, February 1987

Printed in the United States of America

A publication of Loizeaux Brothers, Inc.
A nonprofit organization devoted to the Lord's work
and to the spread of His truth.

Library of Congress Cataloging-in-Publication Data
Strauss, Lehman.
    Listen! our dying Saviour speaks.
    Previously published as: The day God died. 1966.
    Bibliography: p.
    Includes index.
    1. Jesus Christ–Seven last words–Sermons.
2. Baptists–Sermons. 3. Sermons, American.
1. Title.
BT456.S7 1987   232.9'635   86-21460
ISBN 0-87213-828-3

This book was originally published by Zondervan
Publishing House, Grand Rapids, Michigan under the
title, *The Day God Died.*

CONTENTS

INTRODUCTION

CARLYLE CALLED language "the garment of thought." It is true that we can know the inner thinking of a man as he expresses himself in words, "for out of the abundance of the heart the mouth speaketh" (Matthew 12:34). The Bible says further, "To every thing there is a season . . . a time to keep silence, and a time to speak" (Ecclesiastes 3:1, 7). How sad and tragic it has been and still is, that we weak mortals have done so much damage with words! Too frequently, when silence would have been golden, some of us have displayed our ignorance by speaking.

But one Man crossed the stage of human history who was perfect in all His words as well as His ways and works. That Man was Jesus Christ. On one occasion the chief priests and Pharisees sent officers to arrest Him, but they returned to their leaders without Him, and said, "Never man spake like this man" (John 7:46). Instead of arresting Him they were arrested by what He said. His speech was as no other man's. He only could say, "The words that I speak unto you, they are spirit, and they are life" (John 6:63). Unlike our tongues, His was never an unruly evil, full of deadly poison (James 3:8). Christ claimed for His own words that supreme authority and full revelation of God the Father, when He said, "Heaven and earth shall pass away, but my words shall not pass away" (Matthew 24:35).

We commence here a study of our Lord's last sayings on earth uttered from the cross before He died. The Saviour's utterances at Calvary were seven in number . . . no more, no less.

His words were neither too few nor too many. The number seven, in Scripture, suggests the idea of completeness, so that we have here a complete interpretation of the love of God for mankind. The last words of some of the world's greatest men and women have been recorded in books, engraved upon marble slabs and monuments, woven into expensive tapestry, and painted in the most imperishable colors of art. But of all the words that have been preserved for us from the lips of renowned and little-known men, the seven sayings of the Saviour from the cross stand uniquely preeminent, towering high above them all. As He spoke from Golgotha's brow, He used sublime and holy words as the garment of His thought.

Of these seven words of our Lord, three were addressed to God the Father and four to men. I like to think of these seven sayings as seven windows through which we are able to look into the very mind and heart of God. On that darkest day in human history man needed windows through which the light of God could shine. Blessed be His holy Name, that light did shine! And praise God the light is still shining and ever will shine. And wherever these sayings of the Saviour are retold, men are privileged to peer into the mind of the world's Creator and Redeemer and see the heart of the Christian Gospel.

Chapter 1

CHRIST'S IMPERATIVE

A. THE NATURE OF HIS DEATH

B. THE NECESSITY OF HIS DEATH

Chapter 1

CHRIST'S IMPERATIVE

EVERY GENERATION of the Christian Church has recognized the fact of the death of Jesus Christ. It has been incorporated into its preaching and prayers, its creeds and cantatas, its hymns and holy days. When Christendom contemplates its calendar year, the sufferings and sacrifice of our Lord at Calvary are never left out of the plans. Such an omission would be unthinkable. The Church has in a measure always believed in Christ's death.

It has been my good pleasure to read some fine sermons and studies based on the sayings of our Saviour on the cross, and I would suppose that more sermons have been preached each year during "Holy Week" on this theme than on any other. But at the risk of sounding critical, I must say that too often the real meaning and mission of Christ's death is neglected by ministers. They major on Christ's sayings but they minimize His sufferings and substitionary sacrifice. What our Lord said is important, but what He accomplished in His death is indispensable to man's redemption. So then, before we pursue our study of the words of the Redeemer, let us consider first the work of redemption as seen in Christ's death.

A. The Nature of His Death

It is of the highest importance that we understand exactly who it was who suffered and spoke on that cross. In the midst of diversified doctrines about the Person of Christ, it is good that we should ever remind our hearts that the Man who died at Calvary was unlike any other man in human history. And let it be clearly stated that Jesus Christ is not unique merely because of what He said, though His teachings are the greatest. His uniqueness lay in the all-important fact of His absolute Deity. Christ is God! The Cross, the Church, and Christianity are Christocentric. Different convictions about Jesus Christ make the difference between the Trinitarian and the Unitarian. The difference which divides Christendom at this hour might appear to some to be a minor one, but you can be certain it is major and of the highest importance.

Exactly who is this man who spoke from Calvary? I propose an examination of the Holy Scriptures to determine the correct answer to this all-important question. And if one of my readers as much as suggests that the Bible is not the reliable source of accurate information about this question, then I can only conclude that there is no common denominator from which we can proceed agreeably. The great cleavage in Christendom has been created by a difference of belief as to the true seat of authority. The watchword of historic Christianity is the authority of the Holy Scriptures.

First, who was it who came into the world when Jesus Christ was born of Mary? Whatever the complex thoughts of religious leaders on this question, the Bible does spell out the answer with unmistakable clarity. Take first those divinely inspired words as penned by the Apostle John,

> In the beginning was the Word [Christ], and the Word [Christ] was with God, and the Word [Christ] was God.
> And the Word [Christ] was made flesh, and dwelt among us, (and we beheld his glory, the glory as of the only begotten of the Father,) full of grace and truth (John 1:1, 14).

This passage states a truth concerning the Person of Christ, the importance of which cannot be overemphasized. These verses contain one continuous and complete statement, simple yet sublime. They are telling us that the ageless and eternal God came into time and to a place in the form and likeness of a man. I do not comprehend the full meaning of all of this, but I know it is so. Here the eternal pre-existence of the *Logos* is implied, and it is He who became flesh. Thus we are introduced to the God-Man, Jesus Christ, who in substance and essence is truly God and truly man.

Take, next, the divinely inspired words as penned by Paul,

> For in him dwelleth all the fulness of the Godhead bodily (Colossians 2:9).

The writer is not at this point speaking of some mythical person, but of Jesus Christ the Man in whose body dwells all the fullness of the Godhead. The word *Godhead*, as used here (not as used in Romans 1:20) suggests absolute Godhead, full Deity as is found in no other man. Paul is not saying that in Christ dwells a spark of divinity, but rather in Him is full Deity, the *pleroma*, the totality, the sum total of Deity. All that God is we find in the Person of Jesus Christ, "bodily." Mark that word "bodily," for it literally means corporeally, that is, in a material body.

Now if you ask me to explain how this can be, I can only answer you that it rises above the power of human explanation. "Without controversy great is the mystery of godliness: God was manifest in the flesh . . ." (I Timothy 3:16). Here the pre-existence and Incarnation of Deity are asserted. Jesus Christ is both God and Man; He is the God-Man, and at no time during His life on earth, nor since, was He ever less than God. Wherever men have departed from this basic and essential truth, the enemy of Christianity has done his worst. In His birth and through all of His life on earth Christ was God manifest in flesh. This is at one time both the mystery and miracle of the Incarnation.

Now let us move on to the death of this Man, the God-Man, the Word made flesh, the One in whom dwells all the fullness of the Godhead bodily, God manifest in flesh. Was Christ any less God in His death than what He was in His birth and earthly life? The Bible has the answer.

> And all things are of God, who hath reconciled us to himself by Jesus Christ . . . *God was in Christ,* reconciling the world unto himself . . . (II Corinthians 5:18, 19).

The sense of this passage is that, when God effected reconciliation through the death of Christ, "God was in Christ." In His death, as in His virgin birth, Christ is the true "Emmanuel, which being interpreted is, *God with us*" (Matthew 1:23). When God made atonement for the sins of the world through the death of His Son, He was in Christ. At no time did Christ ever lay aside His essential Deity. At no time did He become less than God. And when He comes again He will appear as "the great God and our Saviour Jesus Christ; Who gave himself [on the cross] for us [our sins], that he might redeem us . . ." (Titus 2:13, 14). He was the God-Man in His birth, life, death and resurrection; He is the God-Man in heaven at present; and when He comes again, it will be as that same God-Man. Unless God Himself makes atonement for the sins of the world, there can be no reconciliation of the sinner to Himself. So we conclude that in the Person of Christ, the God-Man died.

That the death of the Second Person in the Godhead was not that of a mere man is pointed out in another passage,

> Take heed therefore unto yourselves, and to all the flock, over the which the Holy Ghost hath made you overseers, to feed the church of God, which he hath purchased with *his own blood* (Acts 20:28).

Here is another of those profound statements in Scripture which treats of the subject of Deity and humanity in the same Person — "the church of God, which he hath purchased with his own blood." I have read that there are those men and women in the medical profession who insist that the blood in a newly conceived baby gets its start from the male sperm. Now we know that Jesus did not have a human father, for before ever Joseph and Mary came together, "she was found with child of the Holy Ghost" (Matthew 1:18). The words "came together" have reference to the physical union of a man and a woman whereby pregnancy would occur. But Mary's pregnancy was before she and Joseph came together. This raises the question in the enquiring medical mind as to the source of Christ's blood. If a human father is necessary for that new life, and the life is in the blood, and since Jesus was conceived in a virgin's womb, then where did He get His blood? The inspired words from Dr. Luke's pen give to us a partial answer at least. That blood was *"His* [God's] *own blood."* The God who gave blood to the first man who was not born of a woman, likewise gave His blood to the God-Man who had no human father. Because Scripture nowhere else makes mention of the blood of God, this verse has presented a difficult textual problem for scholars and critics. But I accept it for what it says. The blood in Christ's body was God's own blood, and since Christ is the God-Man, on the cross it was that divine blood which was shed for our sins. In His death He was no less God than He was in His birth and life. I do not shrink from the thought of the death of Deity since this is the way God planned it.

Throughout the Bible atonement is connected with blood (Exodus 30:10; Leviticus 16:27; Numbers 35:33). Whenever the expiation of sin is in question, it is by means of blood, and wherever the blood is shed, whether in the Old Testament or the New Testament, it signifies essentially death. It is by means of the blood of Christ that we are justified (Romans 5:9); redeemed and forgiven (Ephesians 1:7); cleansed from sin (I John 1:7); loosed from our sins (Revelation 1:5). His blood shed at Calvary was God's blood issuing forth from a body specially and uniquely prepared for the purpose of dying in order that sinful men might be saved. God is a righteous God who cannot condone evil, so in order to justify the ungodly, He Himself came in the Person of Jesus Christ to die as the sinner's Substitute.

Yes, my friends, God was at the cross and on the cross. All that human eyes have ever seen of God is in God the Son, and if ever God was seen in Jesus Christ, it was at Calvary.

B. *The Necessity of His Death*

All evangelical Bible scholars will agree that it was necessary for God to become incarnate and give His life a ransom for sinful humanity. The death of Christ was peremptory, obligatory. Both morally and physically He was obliged to die. It was His imperative. His death was no mere accident, nor was it merely an incident; it was divinely planned. Christ was "the Lamb slain from the foundation of the world" (Revelation 13:8). When He was here on earth He referred to His forthcoming death as a "must." And why? Because everything a sinning man needs was to be provided through His death.

All four gospel writers make much of this divine imperative.

Matthew wrote,

> From that time forth began Jesus to shew unto his disciples, how that he *must* go unto Jerusalem, and suffer many things of the elders and chief priests and scribes, and be killed, and be raised again the third day (Matthew 16:21).

Mark says,

> And he began to teach them, that the Son of man *must* suffer many things, and be rejected of the elders, and of the chief priests, and scribes, and be killed, and after three days rise again (Mark 8:31).

Luke continues,

> The Son of man *must* suffer many things, and be rejected of the elders and chief priests and scribes, and be slain, and be raised the third day (Luke 9:22).

John concludes,

> And as Moses lifted up the serpent in the wilderness, even so *must* the Son of man be lifted up (John 3:14, cf. John 12:34).

These verses tell us that the sufferings and death of Christ were necessary, for in no other way could our Lord make atonement for sin. Both Matthew and Mark record the taunt of His enemies when they said, "If thou be the Son of God, come down from the cross" (Matthew 27:40, 41; Mark 15:30, 32). Now we know that He did not come down from the cross, not because He could not but because He would not. One is appalled at the ignorance of the religious leaders when they said, "He saved others; himself he cannot save." Had these men been possessed of any spiritual understanding at all, they would have known that the Saviour, in order to save others, must be willing not to save Himself. The whole truth of the matter is, He saved others because He would not save Himself. His death was a divine imperative.

The human heart remains unchanged. Men still look upon this great doctrine of the Atonement as a religion of the shambles. They fail to see the Scriptural teaching that the death of Christ was an act of divine impulse. God the Son was one with God the Father in the divine determination to rescue sinners from judgment and hell. The story of redemption is so overwhelming, it should cause every one of us to fall on his face and thank God that He remained on that cross.

When those Jewish leaders said, Come down from the cross and we will believe in you, they displayed extraordinary stupidity. General Booth of Salvation Army fame once said, "It is because Jesus did not come down from the cross that we do believe in Him." The death of God the eternal Son was absolutely necessary. As you read this message and meditate upon Christ's death, remember that here is displayed "love without a limit." There was no limit to the love of God. See your Saviour on yonder cross, and then say, "God loves me like that."

In this opening chapter I have attempted to point out the nature and necessity of Christ's death which I believe to be a preliminary must to a study of His words from the cross. Having seen something of the imperativeness of His sacrifice, we should be better able to understand the importance of His sayings.

It was necessary for Christ to die for the sinner's *pardon*. To commit sin is no small act. And you and I must confess, if we are honest, that we are guilty of having done wrong. We have sinned in our thought processes, in our speech and by our deeds. Now we know that every sin is an offense against God, and that "the wages of sin is death" (Romans 6:23). Therefore we cannot shrug off our wrongdoing and conclude that everything will be all right. Let us face the fact that it is all wrong, and unless we receive pardon from God there is a price which must be paid by the sinner. Now pardon has been provided by God through the death of Jesus Christ, "in whom we have redemption through his blood, the forgiveness of sins, according to the riches of his grace" (Ephesians 1:7). Our pardon, then, is "through his blood." Mark you, it is not through His words, but through His work, that pardoning work which He accomplished through His substitutionary death at Calvary. God cannot excuse sin on any other ground, so, "Let the wicked forsake his way, and the unrighteous man his thoughts: and let him return unto the LORD, and he will have mercy upon him; and to our God, for he will abundantly pardon" (Isaiah 55:7).

It was necessary for Christ to die for the sinner's *peace*. The absence of peace between God and the sinner is the result of unpardoned sin. There can be no peace as long as sin is unforgiven. Pardon is a necessary requisite to peace between God and man. The enmity which exists between God and man grows out of the carnal mind of man, "because the carnal mind is enmity against God: for it is not subject to the law of God, neither indeed can be" (Romans 8:7). The reason for this estrangement is sin. Sin creates disharmony with God, and until the sin has been forgiven the alienation must continue. The greatest discovery the sinner can make is that if he is to have perfect peace he must find his way into harmony with God. Now banish from your mind any idea that you, by your own effort, can make your peace with God. I must bring you back to the Word of God. Study carefully the following words: "For it pleased the Father that in him [Christ] should all fulness dwell; And, having made peace through the blood of his cross, by him to reconcile all things unto himself . . ." (Colossians 1:19, 20). The divine fullness, the *pleroma*, the totality of Deity was in the God-Man in order that He should *make peace through the blood of his cross.* "Therefore being justified by faith, we have peace with God through our Lord Jesus

Christ" (Romans 5:1). The soul that trusts the death of Christ for pardon will have peace with God.

It was necessary for Christ to die for the sinner's *purity*. The absence of purity in the sinner is the result of unpardoned sin and an estrangement from God. Thus far we have tried to show that the death of Jesus Christ was the death of the God-Man, and that He effected pardon and peace for sinners, not by His sayings but by His substitutionary sacrifice; not by His verbal deliberations but by His vicarious death. But mere pardon and peace would leave us incomplete, and by saying this I do not intend to undervalue divine pardon. I simply propose to add that the death of Christ goes deeper. It provides for the believing sinner an inner consciousness, that acute awareness that he no longer is an offense to God. Here is my text:

> How much more shall the blood of Christ, who through the eternal Spirit offered himself without spot to God, purge your conscience from dead works to serve the living God (Hebrews 9:14).

Dr. G. Campbell Morgan uses the word "consciousness" instead of "conscience." I think it is a good replacement both exegetically and experientially. The believing sinner who receives pardon and peace also receives a pure consciousness of things, something he did not possess before he was saved. The unsaved person has a keener awareness of the impure rather than the pure, while the saved man has a keener awareness of the pure rather than the impure. Instead of a defiled consciousness the child of God now knows deliverance from defilement, and his desires are toward his Deliverer. And what effected the change? Certainly it was not the Law of God, but the love of God which was commended toward us, "in that, while we were yet sinners, Christ died for us" (Romans 5:8).

It was necessary for Christ to die for the sinner's *power*. The Christian has pardon, peace and purity, but he is not beyond the possibility of peril. He is not immune from the temptations to think, speak and act wrongly. In order to live victoriously over sin he needs power. Being a Christian in this life does not remove me from the possibility of sinning. Now the teachings of Christ as to right and wrong are the finest, but His teachings alone will not enable you and me to triumph over the power of sin. We will admit to this if we are honest. No less a saint than the Apostle Paul testified, "For I know that in me (that is, in my flesh,) dwelleth no good thing . . . when I would do good, evil is present with me" (Romans 7:18, 21). We are constantly in a conflict, and at times we find ourselves yielding to wrong, and that in spite of the fact that the sayings of the Saviour are with us still. We study His precepts but they do not provide the necessary power to obey them. The power to overcome evil will not come to us through His expositions, but rather through His expiration. And now, I must give you my text:

> For the Word of the cross is . . . unto us which are being saved . . . the power of God (I Corinthians 1:18).

You will notice that I have not used the King James Version. The tense of the verb is translated more accurately, "being saved," not "saved." Now it is true that we Christians have been saved, that is, we have been saved from the penalty of sin (Ephesians 2:8). And we are just as certain that we shall be saved, that is, we shall be saved from the possibility of sin (Romans 5:9). The first of these is past; the second is in prospect; but what about the present? We have been saved from the penalty of sin, and we shall be saved from the possibility of sin, but are we being saved now from the practice of sin? Our text tells us that if we are being saved, it is the word of the cross which is the power of God for this salvation. The eternal Word of the cross enables the sinner to find salvation from the penalty of sin, but that same eternal word will likewise provide power to live victoriously over sin. Notice that it is not the preaching of the cross, but the *Logos*, the Word, the same Word who became flesh, in whom dwelt all the fullness of the Godhead and Who died on the cross. It is not our aim in this series of studies to merely examine the words of a man who hung dying on a cross, but the words of *the* Word. When we come to the end of our own resources, realizing that we cannot do without Him, then it is that He works His power in and through us. Believe me when I tell you that He is sufficient for all you will ever need in this life, even for that necessary power to live victoriously over sin.

Finally, it was necessary for Christ to die for the sinner's *prospect.* "If in this life only we have hope in Christ, we are of all men most miserable" (I Corinthians 15:19). There is no bright prospect in a religion whose founder lies dead. Those two disciples on the way to Emmaus have testified to this. After our Lord's crucifixion they made their way in utter despair. Luke says they were "sad" (Luke 24:17). What made them sad? The answer is clear. They said, "We trusted [past tense] that it had been he which should have redeemed Israel: and beside all this, today is the third day since all these things were done" (Luke 24:21). The prospect they once had was now gone from them, and all because of their own foolish and faithless hearts (Luke 24:25). Actually they knew better than they believed.

Turn back with me to those three *musts* in the synoptic gospels earlier in this chapter, and there you will find Christ's bodily Resurrection from the grave linked inseparably with His death (Matthew 16:21; Mark 8:31; Luke 9:22). The believer's prospect is not in our Lord's death alone but also in His Resurrection. When the Christian Gospel is defined by Paul, the bodily Resurrection of Christ is an integral part of it. The apostle writes, "I declare unto you the gospel . . . how that Christ died for our sins according to the scriptures; and that he was buried, and that he arose again the third day according to the scriptures" (I Corinthians 15:1-4).

Our prospect for the future is in our resurrected Lord. But He needed to die first before He could rise from the dead. He "was delivered for our offences, and was raised again for our justification" (Romans 4:25). "Blessed be the God and Father of our Lord Jesus Christ, which according to his abundant mercy hath begotten us again unto a lively hope by the resurrection of Jesus Christ from the dead" (I Peter 1:3).

Chapter **2**

THE FIRST WORD

CHRIST'S INTERCESSION

Then said Jesus, Father, forgive them;
for they know not what they do . . .
— Luke 23:34

A. THE BLINDING PROPENSITIES OF SIN

B. THE BLESSED PROVISION FOR SIN

Chapter 2

CHRIST'S INTERCESSION

Then said Jesus, Father, forgive them;
for they know not what they do . . .
— Luke 23:34

DRAWING NEAR to the dying Saviour, we catch a glimpse of the great burden of His heart. There was no resentment there, else He would have uttered imprecations on those who had inflicted His sufferings. There was no self-pity or self-ishness, else He would have appealed to His tormentors for clemency and consideration. It will be to our advantage to move slowly, listening intently to each word, lest we fail to lay hold of their fullest significance.

His first word was "Father," and it tells us that, in spite of all through which He had passed and of that which He was enduring at that moment, He possessed that abiding consciousness of His eternal Sonship. Under staggering losses and severe crosses, when right is being suppressed and wrong is triumphing, faith is tempted to doubt that God is still dealing with us as a Father, but rather that He is dealing with us as a Judge. Yet never once did our Lord fail to avail Himself of the blessed relationship between the Father and Himself. It is significant that His public ministry commenced with prayer to the Father (Luke 3:21), and now we see Him on the cross concluding His ministry with prayer. During His brief stay on the earth He sometimes spent a whole night in prayer. And now at the last, amidst His deepest sorrow, He enters the prayer chamber again. And blessing of blessings, we are permitted to listen as He speaks to the Father.

I cannot think of any relationship on earth more satisfying than a wholesome father-son relationship, with each having confidence in the other. I recall those tender moments in the lives of my young sons as we talked things over and prayed together at the end of the day. They were times of precious fellowship as each in his childish way revealed and expressed what was in his mind and heart. And then I recall those times of discussion and counsel as those early influences were to mature into the decisions of great importance, finding God's will for their lives, continuing their education, choosing their life partners. This door of fellowship remains open between us and I trust will remain open as long as we live. It is vital to both of us.

For Christians, Christ gives a perfect example on the cross of a precious ministry that can be performed in behalf of others when there is nothing else that one can do. If one is incapacitated, and his hands and feet can do nothing to serve others, that one can pray. God has allowed many a saint of His to linger on a bed of illness for the specific purpose of engaging in a ministry of prayer, and I do not doubt that much has been accomplished through such intercession. Child of God, let not one of us ever regard himself as being beyond usefulness. If we cannot attend meetings, give out tracts, teach a Sunday school class, preach, or write a book, we can all pray as long as we are conscious.

Looking now at our Lord's intercession, two tremendous thoughts appear quite clearly.

A. *The Blinding Propensities of Sin*

In His prayer Christ said, *"They know not what they do."* Of what were they ignorant? Certainly they were not ignorant of the fact that they were crucifying a good and innocent man. Pilate bore witness to this when he said, "I, having examined him before you, have found no fault in this man touching those things whereof ye accuse him: No, nor yet Herod: for I sent you to him; and, lo, nothing worthy of death is done unto him" (Luke 23:14, 15). When the Jews discovered that Pilate, following his usual custom of releasing a prisoner at the feast (Mark 15:6), was planning to release Jesus, they howled him down and demanded the release of Barabbas. The mob knew, and Judas knew, that Christ had done nothing worthy of death. No, they were not ignorant of the fact that they were putting to death an innocent man. The entire trial was a miscarriage of justice.

Of what, then, were they ignorant? They knew not that they were crucifying the Lord of glory. Paul echoed that fact of their ignorance when he wrote of that "Which none of the princes of this world knew: for had they known it, they would not have crucified the Lord of glory" (I Corinthians 2:8). After the crucifixion, Peter said, "And now brethren, I wot that through ignorance ye did it, as did also your rulers" (Acts 3:17). For all their sin against light, there was an actual blindness as to the real Person and purpose of Jesus Christ. Neither Peter nor Paul soft-pedaled their sermons, yet both recognized a certain blindness on the part of Christ's enemies. Because Christ was so different from what they hoped the Messiah would be, they were not aware of the awful criminality of their conduct.

The most abysmal ignorance in the world today is the ignorance of worldly-wise men about spiritual things. Every day man discovers some new thing about God's creation, and yet he knows so little about God. We see even today the blinding propensity of sin. Think of the unbelieving Jew! "Their minds were blinded: for until this day remaineth the same veil untaken away in the reading of the old testament; which veil is done away in Christ" (II Corinthians 3:14). Think of the unbelieving Gentile! "In whom the god of this world hath blinded the minds of them which believe not, lest the light of the glorious gospel of Christ, who is the image of God, should shine unto them" (II Corinthians 4:4).

In these days when "knowledge shall increase" and has increased, one has only to turn to the great technological advances in any field of science known to find that spiritual insight has not increased in the same proportion as natural insight. Some of these great scientific secrets rest in the minds of unbelievers. With all their keen insight in the whys and hows of things, these men remain spiritually blind.

This is not true of all the intelligentsia. I think of General Lew Wallace, of the United States Army, who with all his brilliant career and intellectual prowess, sought to read the Bible carefully to prove it was a sham. Instead, the scales of his blindness fell away, he saw his shame, and accepted Christ as his Saviour.

Count Leo Tolstoy, Russian writer, testifies, "For thirty-five years of my life I was, in the proper acceptance of the word, a nihilist — a man who believed nothing. Five years ago I believed in the doctrines of Jesus, and my whole life underwent a sudden transformation."

One who did not remain in intellectual blindness was the Right Hon. Sir A. J. Balfour, British statesman and essayist. He wrote, "Christ is a rare jewel, but men know not His value; a sun which ever shines, but men perceive not His brightness nor walk in His light. He is a garden full of sweets, a hive full of honey, a sun without a spot, a star ever bright, a fountain ever full, a brook which ever flows, a rose which ever blooms, a foundation which never yields, a guide who never errs, a friend who never forsakes."

But of you who read this message it never can be said, "They know not what they do." In our day of advanced education and widespread distribution of the Gospel, there is a certain willful ignorance on the part of many. Of course this condition has always existed. Man has never lived up to the light God has given to him. The Apostle Peter wrote, "For this they willingly are ignorant of, that by the word of God the heavens were of old, and the earth standing out of the water and in the water" (II Peter 3:5). There are those who have heard the truth and can believe it if they want to believe it. Their unbelief is a willful refusal on their part to accept the truth. And for all such there is no forgiveness unless they turn from their unbelief and receive by faith the Lord Jesus Christ.

And now another truth demands our attention; namely,

B. *The Blessed Provision for Sin*

Our Lord's intercessory prayer continues, *"Father, forgive them."* This first word from the cross reveals Christ as man's Intercessor, and His intercession makes available the mercy of God. The Man dying on that cross was not only the Lamb being led to the slaughter, but also the Mediator for sinners and the High Priest for His own. Glorious thought this! Here we see and hear the Saviour at prayer. At least eight of His prayers are recorded, but this one is unique.

One day He sat on a hillside surrounded by the beauty of a lovely landscape, and there He inspired His disciples with the words, "Whosoever shall smite thee on thy right cheek, turn to him the other also," and "Love your enemies, bless them that curse you, do good to them that hate you, and pray for them which despitefully use you, and persecute you" (Matthew 5:39, 44). These were stirring and thought-provoking words.

On another occasion one of His disciples sought His viewpoint on the matter of forgiveness. "Then came Peter to him, and said, Lord, how oft shall my brother sin against me, and I forgive him? till seven times? Jesus saith unto him, I say not unto thee, Until seven times: but, Until seventy times seven" (Matthew 18:21, 22). Our Lord was not giving to Peter a lesson in mathematics; He was telling him to just keep on forgiving.

There on the cross, in full possession of His faculties, Christ practiced what He preached. His teachings were no mere impractical sentiments; they were the divine standards for everyday living, and at Calvary He demonstrated the lesson of forgiveness. There were His tormentors, His persecutors, His murderers; but He prayed for them all. He perfectly exemplified His own teaching and left us an example that we should follow in His steps (I Peter 2:21). If those who trespass against us repent of their wrong, we are obliged to forgive them (Luke 17:3, 4), but even if they do not repent and seek our forgiveness, we must continue to pray for them.

Was our Lord's prayer answered? The answer to this question can be had only as we understand that for which He prayed. Be it known that this prayer was not a request for God to wink at ignorance, nor was it a request for the blanket pardon of the sins of His murderers. To be certain His prayer was not a petition asking God to thrust forgiveness upon men who did not want His forgiveness. Russell Bradley Jones wrote, "When He said, 'Father, forgive *them*,' the unexpressed implication is clearly, 'And condemn *Me*.' For only by assuming their debt could He plead for their forgiveness. In this appeal He was isolating Himself as the world's only Saviour. He was saying to the Father, 'Charge their wrong doing to My account.'"[1]

Yes, His prayer was answered. God did not strike down those poor deceived and deluded ignoramuses. On and after the day of Pentecost they learned what the cross was about, and our Saviour's prayer was answered. Luke wrote, "And now, brethren, I wot that through ignorance ye did it, as did also your rulers . . . Repent ye therefore, and be converted, that your sins may be blotted out . . ." (Acts 3:17, 19). Many were saved in that day because God's wrath was not poured out upon those sinners at Calvary. And many have been saved since because the day of grace has remained open for all and will remain so until our Lord Jesus Christ returns for His own.

As I sat preparing this message to be preached the following day at a special Good Friday service, my telephone rang. My caller inquired as to what I intended to preach about the next day. When I gave him my text (Luke 23:34), he informed me that he would not bother to attend inasmuch as I had chosen a text that was not inspired. He said that Luke was not an eyewitness to the crucifixion and that the only statements we can be certain that Christ spoke on the cross are to be found in the gospel according to John. Then he proceeded to ask me why Christ did not forgive His murderers Himself instead of asking His Father to forgive them. His inference was, of course, that my text cast aspersions on Christ's power to forgive sins.

Now we know that hitherto our Lord forgave men Himself and did not intercede to the Father to do so (see Matthew 9:2; Luke 7:48). Moreover, we agree that forgiving sin is a divine prerogative (Mark 2:7). Why then did Christ call upon the Father to forgive sin? I have found no more satisfying answer

[1] Jones, Russell Bradley, *Gold From Golgotha* (Grand Rapids: Baker Book House, 1957), p. 16.

than that given by the late Arthur W. Pink. He wrote, "Mark carefully His own words, and then behold the marvelous accuracy of Scripture. He had said, 'The Son of Man hath power *on earth* to forgive sins' (Matthew 9:6). But He was no longer on earth! He had been lifted *from the earth* (John 12:32)! Moreover, on the cross He was acting as our Substitute; the Just was about to die for the unjust. Hence, it was, that hanging there as our Representative, He was no longer in the place of authority where He might exercise His own divine prerogatives, therefore He takes the position of a suppliant before the Father." [2]

When Christ comes into a life, that person becomes a new creature; but nowhere does this new life stand out more noticeably than among those who at one time lived in open sin. Such was Teresa, a veritable little "river rat" that Mrs. Van Eddings of the Orinoco River Mission tells of. Without the Gospel of Christ and His transforming power with the forgiveness of sins, Teresa could have continued to live just like all the rest of the little "river rats," existing without any moral code.

As Teresa began to take on the form of young womanhood, she began to be the object of the coveting eyes of lustful men who wanted to have her in unabashed sin. But then Christ found her and she became a new creature in Him.

The way was hard at first. She smelled so much of the river — creeping things in her hair and a lust for the missionaries' household items in her heart. But she demonstrated real sorrow for her sin and a genuine love for the Lord, so that when provided with help, she grew up into Christ.

When the call came for someone to take the Gospel to her own people, she responded. With a heart full of gratitude to God for the forgiveness of her sins, she continued to be ra-

[2] Pink, Arthur W., *The Seven Sayings of Our Saviour on the Cross* (Grand Rapids: Baker Book House).

diantly happy. Christ had changed the life of a little river rat into that of "The King's daughter — all glorious within."

Sir George Williams of London, founder of the Y.M.C.A., testified, "I cannot describe to you the joy and peace which flowed into my soul when I saw that the Lord Jesus had died for my sins, and that they were all forgiven through simple faith in His precious blood."

Man needs forgiveness for his sins, whether those sins were committed wittingly or unwittingly; and the forgiveness must be preceded by a blood sacrifice (Leviticus 5:15, 16; Numbers 15:22-25). Christ is that Sacrifice. It is only as men turn to Him that God can forgive them. In answer to Christ's prayer the Day of Judgment has been postponed now for nineteen hundred years. Divine power has been holding back the gates of hell while divine grace has been helping poor sinners find their way to God. However, the postponement does not mean escape for anyone. If you refuse to come to God through faith in the Lord Jesus Christ, you are lost forever. You can obtain God's forgiveness now by accepting God's Substitute.

Chapter **3**

CHRIST'S INTERVENTION

*And Jesus said unto him, Verily I say
unto thee, To day shalt thou be with
me in paradise.* —Luke 23:43

A. The Request of the Dying Sinner

B. The Response of the Divine Saviour

Chapter 3

THE SECOND WORD

CHRIST'S INTERVENTION

And Jesus said unto him, Verily I say unto thee, To day shalt thou be with me in paradise. —Luke 23:43

IN THE FIRST WORD our whole attention is drawn to our Lord alone. No other human voice is heard that might have prompted the prayer He offered to the Father. It was a request for His enemies — all of them. In that prayer He fulfilled perfectly the office of Mediator and High Priest. He not only offered Himself as the sacrifice for sin, but He prayed for sinners. What our Lord said and did here harmonize perfectly with the divinely inspired word from the pen of the Apostle Paul, where we read, "For there is one God, and one mediator between God and men, the man Christ Jesus" (I Timothy 2:5).

No one can study the seven words from the cross without being impressed with the close relation between the first word and the second word. The first word was a prayer for His enemies. The second word was an answer to that prayer. The forgiveness for which He prayed is now to be extended to one repentant sinner. The dying thief became the first fruits of our Lord's intercessory prayer for sinners.

A student once asked why only one was saved in view of the fact that Christ prayed for them all. We are not certain that the dying thief was the only one who was saved at that time. His is the one conversion preserved for the records. We do know that "The Lord . . . is longsuffering to us-ward, not willing that any should perish, but that all should come to repentance" (II Peter 3:9). We know, further, as we shall see in our study of the text, that the one whose salvation is mentioned was saved because he believed in the Lord Jesus Christ as his own personal Saviour from sin's guilt and penalty. Why was not the other thief saved? You tell me why it is that under exactly the same conditions, some are melted and moved to receive Jesus Christ and others remain unmoved and indifferent. I only know that a man must believe on the Lord Jesus Christ to be saved and that God will save all who do believe.

What did Christ mean when He said, "And I, if I be lifted up from the earth, will draw all men unto me" (John 12: 32)? Certainly, He was referring to His death, for the verse which follows says, "This he said, signifying what death he should die" (verse 33).

But this verse does not say that all men will be saved. Nor can we say with any amount of dogmatism exactly what our Lord did mean. We do know, however, that ever since the day of His crucifixion, the whole world has been drawn to Him in the matter of time. His death divided all of history. We indicate time to be either before Christ (B.C.) or in the year of our Lord, *anno Domini* (A.D.). The editors of every daily newspaper throughout the world, the writer of every letter, the signer of every check, all are drawn to Him. All do not recognize Him and receive Him as their Saviour and Lord, but in that one respect all are drawn to Him as the determiner of time for them. And because He was lifted up on the cross, and later in His Resurrection and Ascension, He will be lifted up again and all men will be drawn to Him when He comes back to earth, when "every knee should bow . . . and every tongue should confess that Jesus Christ is Lord, to the glory of God the Father" (Philippians 2:10, 11).

Returning now to the incident of the dying thief, we see a strong Scriptural refutation of some of the most dangerous heresies that have crept into Christendom. All forms of sacramentalism such as baptism, the Lord's Supper, church membership and good works, as necessary to salvation, are here refuted. Here the dogma of purgatory, the notion of soul-sleep, the teaching of universalism, all are disproved. Dr. Charles R. Erdman said, "The story of the penitent thief has sometimes been considered the most surprising, the most suggestive, the most instructive incident in all Gospel narrative."

Why did God allow His beloved Son, His only begotten Son, His holy and perfect Son to be crucified between two criminals? Be certain God did have a reason. One need only read Isaiah 53 to find the answer. The death of Jesus Christ had to demonstrate all of the despicable shame, sorrow and penalty attached to sin and Adam's fall. Then, too, the Prophet said, "He was numbered among the transgressors" (Isaiah 53: 12, cf. Mark 15:28 and Luke 22:37).

A. The Request of the Dying Sinner

"And he said unto Jesus, Lord, remember me when thou comest into thy kingdom" (Luke 23:42). Tradition holds that the penitent thief was being put to death for insurrection and that his name was Dysmas. He is a representative case, an example of what a man feels and believes and confesses in order to be saved. That there was no essential difference between the two thieves is seen from the divine record as recorded by Matthew. Both are said to have reviled our Lord (Matthew 27:44).

But one of them repented, and being gripped with the fear of God, he confessed that there was justice in the punishment he was receiving but injustice in the treatment of the Nazarene. Said he, "We indeed justly; for we receive the due reward of our deeds: but this man hath done nothing amiss" (Luke 23:41). An important revelation is this – the sinfulness of man and the sinlessness of Jesus Christ! Their crosses were common. Their deaths were common. Yet there was one thing they did not have in common. The thieves were sinners suffering for their own sins; the God-Man on the middle cross was the sinless One suffering for the sins of others. Here are two basic elements essential to salvation. If a man does not see his own sin and guilt, he will not sense the need for salvation. Moreover, if Jesus Christ is not the sinless One, then He is powerless to save others.

Only recently I read once again the account of the conversion of the late Dr. Percy B. Crawford, one of America's greatest youth evangelists. As a boy he had gone often to Sunday school and church, but never did he know in those early years a sense of guilt and of the lostness of his condition. Some years later, as a young man, he attended the Church of the Open Door in Los Angeles and heard a guest preacher who was supplying the pulpit in the absence of Dr. Reuben A. Torrey. As the Word of God was faithfully and forcefully proclaimed, the Holy Spirit spoke conviction to the heart of young Percy Crawford. When the invitation was given, he walked forward at the suggestion of a personal worker, and that day he surrendered to Jesus Christ. Undoubtedly there were others among the thousands present at that service who were convicted of sin but who were not saved. Some of you will ask me, Why? My answer is, I do not know. Permit me to ask you a question. Why is it that some of you who read this message might still be unsaved? Certainly Christ is able to save you. And you can be saved now if you will decide for Christ.

Our Lord was in wretched company in that hour of His death. His crucifixion was a grimly spectacular scene. He was placed among criminals who had been taken from the jail at Jerusalem. The synoptic gospels make much of Christ's reputation as a man who mingled among sinners (Matthew 9:10-13; 11:19; Mark 2:15, 16; Luke 5:30; 7:34; 15:2; 19:7). He never denied these charges. And now in his dying moments He is found with them. Why? He said, "For I am not come to call the righteous, but sinners to repentance" (Matthew 9:13; Mark 2:17; Luke 5:32). Had the unrepentant thief taken his place as a sinner, as did his companion, he too would have been saved.

The penitent, when addressing the Son of God, said, "*Jesus, Lord . . .*" By divine revelation he saw in Mary's Son both the human and the divine. It was by divine decree that He was named "*Jesus*" at His Incarnation (Matthew 1:21). It was His personal name, meaning, "Jehovah is the Saviour." Jesus came into the world to identify Himself with sinners in order that He might save them (Luke 19:10). "Thou shalt call his name Jesus: for he shall save his people from their sins" (Matthew 1:21).

He not only witnessed to his faith in the *sinlessness* and *saviourhood* of Jesus, but he confessed also His *sovereignty*. He called Jesus, "Lord." Wherever there is a sense of who Jesus is, there is a sense of sin. If He is merely Jesus the man, then He cannot be the Saviour. But wherever His Lordship is believed, and by this I mean His absolute Deity, there you will find a work of salvation going on in someone's heart. If Jesus is not God, then He is powerless to save. God only can forgive sins (Mark 2:7), and that is exactly what Jesus the Lord did when He said, "The Son of man hath power on earth to forgive sins" (Matthew 9:6). (See also Luke 5:18-26 and

Luke 7:47-50.) There can be no question but that Jesus is presented in the New Testament as God Incarnate. Christ claimed Deity and He was Deity (John 1:1). His Deity is the test whereby we may distinguish between the true Saviour and false saviours, between the true Messiah and false messiahs. No soul can form a true judgment of the Deity of Christ apart from the power of the Holy Spirit in his life, for "no man can say that Jesus is the Lord, but by the Holy Ghost" (I Corinthians 12:3). "Whosoever believeth that Jesus is the Christ is born of God" (I John 5:1). "That if thou shalt confess with thy mouth the Lord Jesus, and shalt believe in thine heart that God hath raised him from the dead, thou shalt be saved" (Romans 10:9). Of all the attributes of Deity ascribed to Him, His absolute authority, as seen in the title, *Lord,* stands out as a significant one. Indeed the penitent thief had saving faith in Jesus Christ as God.

While visiting the Auca Indians in the jungles of Ecuador, I talked with the once savage killers of those five missionaries of martyr fame. One of those jungle Indians in particular impressed me deeply as having had a genuine experience of Holy Spirit regeneration. With Rachel Saint acting as interpreter, he testified that his faith in Jesus Christ as His Creator and Saviour brought to pass the change in his heart. When he surrendered to Jesus as Lord, the sovereign Saviour rescued him from sin and hell.

Finally, the dying thief believed in Christ's *Resurrection* and *Second Coming.* He prayed, *"Remember me when thou comest into thy kingdom."* Of course, resurrection truth was a part of his faith, for he could not contemplate Christ's return to set up His kingdom unless he believed that the Son of God would rise from the dead. Consider how strong this man's faith was! He had faith in Christ's coming kingdom at a moment when, to all outward appearances, His kingdom was lost. By faith he saw the crown beyond the cross, the sovereignty that was to follow the suffering. He knew that in order to have the Kingdom, there must of necessity be the King.

Can you project yourself into the place of this malefactor? Can you suppose yourself to be present and to be looking upon the dying form of the Man on the middle cross? Do you think you could readily believe Him to be the Lord of Glory, who would return to earth to establish His Kingdom? I leave each of you to answer for yourself. But before you answer, note once more what His disciples did: "Then all the disciples forsook him, and fled" (Matthew 26:56). It was no mean faith that believed in Christ's coming Kingdom in that dark hour.

The Revised Version reads *"in* thy kingdom," in place of the Authorized Version which says, *"into* thy kingdom." It would seem, therefore, that the thief was contemplating a time in the distant future when Jesus would come "in" His Kingdom. Certainly Christ had in mind a future, literal Kingdom when He taught His disciples to pray, "Thy kingdom come" (Matthew 6:10; Luke 11:2). Every kingdom has its king. The Kingdom of Christ will come to earth when He comes back again to be its King. The dying penitent looked away from the sufferings of Christ to the glory that should follow (I Peter 1:11; 4:13; 5:1). Whether or not he understood the nature of Christ's Kingdom, he was offering himself to be a willing subject of the King.

If I did not have the written record of Christ's response to this man, I should expect to meet him in heaven. He believed and confessed Christ under the most extenuating circumstances. He leads the pack in the matter of faith. Some of you were raised in a Christian environment, surrounded by godly parents and a faithful minister of God's Word, and still you are unsaved. This man confessed Christ when no one else was confessing Him, and it was as public a confession as one could make. Spurgeon once said, "If you are nailed to a cross, I do not urge you to be baptized. If you are fastened to a tree, I do not invite you to the Lord's Supper, nor to join a church. But you are required to make as clear and distinct a confession of the Lord Jesus Christ as is suitable to your present condition."

I will not say that there are *many* last minute conversions of suffering and dying sinners; neither will I agree with those who say that there are not *any*. When I was in Decatur, Alabama, the pastor of the church in which I was preaching asked me to accompany him to a hospital to visit an unsaved man who was dying. When I looked at the patient, it seemed obvious to me that he was not long for this life. I told him that God loved him and Christ died to save him and that if he died without Christ he would be lost forever. That day he could not comprehend how God could save him after all the years he had rejected Christ. All our effort appeared for the moment to be in vain. We prayed and left the room. But the days that followed found us praying often for this needy soul. And then on a subsequent visit, the pastor found him with a ready and responsive spirit. He confessed Christ as his Saviour and Lord, gave evidence of becoming a new creature in Christ, and slipped into eternity.

B. *The Response of the Divine Saviour*

"And Jesus said unto him, Verily I say unto thee, To day shalt thou be with me in paradise" (Luke 23:43). Our Lord might have said, "You have waited too long. You lived the life of a wicked man, and now you deserve your fate." But He couldn't say this. Do you know why? Let me tell you. One time Jesus said, "Him that cometh to me I will in no wise cast out" (John 6:37). And that is exactly what the man did. He came to Jesus, not to ask Him to release him from suffering, but to be saved from sin's penalty.

Christ prefaced His reply to the prayer with a *"verily."* The word means *amen.* It is a confirmation, a commitment. He was telling the praying sinner that he could depend upon Christ to grant his request. The *amen* of the Lord Jesus is His seal of approval upon the request. "Verily — so be it, so it is." It was a favorite expression of our Lord's. It is His way of telling the believing sinner that He will not fail one soul who comes to Him. Sometimes He spoke with a twofold assurance by using a double "verily." *"Verily, verily,* I say unto you, He that heareth my word, and believeth on him that sent me, hath everlasting life, and shall not come into condemnation; but is passed from death unto life" (John 5:24).

Our Lord accepted the penitent sinner immediately, thereby showing to us that conversion is sudden and immediate. If conversion were a lengthened process, there would have been no hope for that sinner, nor for any of us. The response of God to the penitent and seeking soul is swift and sure. Divine love needs but an opening to flow into the sin-darkened chambers of a human heart. "Today!" said our Lord. Not after you are baptized, but "Today." Not after you have done penance or passed through a mythical purgatory, but "Today." The grace of God exceeds the fondest expectations of the sinner's heart. When a sinner comes to Christ, he is forgiven and cleansed at once. Jesus said to Zacchaeus, *"This day* is salvation come to this house" (Luke 19:9). There is no probation period for a believing sinner. When the sinner receives the Saviour, there is a new beginning at once.

On December 25, 1927, at three o'clock in the afternoon, I called upon God to save me. I confessed my sin and guilt, received Jesus Christ as my Saviour and Lord, and that moment God saved me. I was there when it happened. I knew then that He had saved me, and I never once doubted from that day to this that I was a child of God. There is no Scriptural ground to make a paradise into a purgatory or a period of probation.

The great blessing of salvation is in Christ's words *"with me."* As the veil in the temple was rent in twain, showing man's access to God through the expiatory sacrifice of Christ, this redeemed thief walked arm in arm with the Son of God into the very presence of the Father. He entered triumphantly through the gates of glory. If there was a sad farewell from loved ones who watched him die, there was a glad welcome in heaven.

Where was he? "Absent from the body . . . present with the Lord" (II Corinthians 5:8). How did he fare? "To depart and to be with Christ . . . is *far better*" (Philippians 1:23). Death to the believer means the immediate presence with his Saviour. Salvation through Christ is union with Christ both in this life and in the life to come. No man could wish for anything more. "So shall we ever be with the Lord" (I Thessalonians 4:17).

Some tell us that following the death of the body, the soul sleeps. The Bible knows nothing of this. Others believe that at death the soul is completely annihilated. This, too, is in direct contradiction to what the Bible teaches. Then there is the theory that the soul becomes something or someone else. This too has no Biblical basis. Jesus said, "Thou shalt be with me." Therein lies the secret of true joy and eternal bliss. And therein lies the victory over the fear and sting of death. I do not need to know any more about life after death than the fact that I shall be "with Christ." To come to Christ in this life is to be with Christ in the life to come. My own heart rejoices at the very thought of the immediacy of being at home with my Lord *today;* not for today only, not for a month only, not for a millennium only, but for all eternity.

"In paradise." The word "paradise" appears only three times in the New Testament. We know that it means the abode

of God, for Jesus' last words were, "Father, into thy hands I commend my spirit" (Luke 23:46). Christ, at His death, having committed His spirit to the Father, went in spirit immediately into heaven, the dwelling place of God. The apostle describes it as "the third heaven" (II Corinthians 12:2-4). It is the heavenly home of the redeemed where one finds the "tree of life" (Revelation 2:7).

Is it possible for a Christian to become too heavenly minded? No! He cannot give too much thought to his eternal home in the life to come. This is the goal, the ultimate of salvation. The great truth contained in this second word of Christ from the cross, aside from the assurance and hope it brought to the penitent thief, is that we too who have trusted the Son of God, shall be with Him.

> The dying thief rejoiced to see
> That fountain in his day;
> And there may I, though vile as he,
> Wash all my sins away.

Chapter 4

THE THIRD WORD

CHRIST'S INTERESTS

*When Jesus therefore saw his mother,
and the disciple standing by, whom he
loved, he saith unto his mother, Woman,
behold thy son! Then saith he to the
disciple, Behold thy mother! . . .*

John 19:26, 27

A. THE END OF A HUMAN RELATIONSHIP

B. THE EXTENT OF HUMAN RESPONSIBILITY

Chapter 4

CHRIST'S INTERESTS

*When Jesus therefore saw his mother,
and the disciple standing by, whom he
loved, he saith unto his mother, Woman,
behold thy son! Then saith he to the
disciple, Behold thy mother! . . .*
                                    John 19:26, 27

LET US NOT forget that we are still at Calvary.
Though the word *Calvary* appears once only in the Bible (Luke
23:33), it stands out in the minds of multiplied millions as the
place where scores of Old Testament prophecies converged for
their final fulfillment. The translators have adopted this word
from the Latin *Calvaria*, meaning a skull. The Greek word
kranion, from *kara*, meaning "a head," gives to us our English
word *cranium*, denoting a skull. Three of the gospel writers
have used the corresponding Aramaic word *Golgotha*, so named
because the hill was skull-like in shape (Matthew 27:33; Mark
15:22; John 19:17). The place where our Lord was crucified
has been referred to often as Mount Calvary. Actually there

is no sanction for this expression since the hill on which Christ died was not more than twenty feet high.

What is significant to us in this series of studies is the fact that from the hill called Calvary, our dying Saviour spoke seven times. In this third word we hear Him speaking to His mother Mary and to John, the beloved disciple. As a matter of fact, His first three words expressed His interest in the needs of mankind. In the awful agony of those dying moments His concern was for others. The best balm for pain and sorrow is to minister to others. Some of us have not yet learned this great lesson of life. We bemoan our sorrows and losses, expecting that all the world will rush to our side with its substance and sympathy. But when we act in such fashion we lose one of life's most valued blessings. When life seems to go to pieces, a sure way of putting it together again is to minister to others. "Blessed be God, even the Father of our Lord Jesus Christ, the Father of mercies, and the God of all comfort; Who comforteth us in all our tribulation, that we may be able to comfort them which are in any trouble, by the comfort wherewith we ourselves are comforted of God" (II Corinthians 1:3, 4).

In His deepest sorrow our Saviour thought first of others, not of Himself. His first word was a prayer for His enemies who hated Him. He interceded on their behalf. His second word was a warm and ready response to the appeal of a criminal who wanted salvation. And now here in His third word He extends to His mother the respect and consideration due her. I cannot imagine a more glorious and triumphant way to die than this; namely, in the extending of one's self in supplying the needs of others. No man dies in vain who blesses others in his expiration.

No doubt there were many bystanders and onlookers who gathered around the cross on that eventful day in history. The majority of them, however, were not sympathizers of the Saviour; they were the critics of the Christ. Amidst the gathering gloom of Golgotha different groups mingled. There were Pharisees, scribes, priests, elders of the people, peasants and even a few Roman officials. A cursory reading of the gospel records reveals the feelings of that crowd. Some "reviled Him" (Matthew 27:39). Others taunted Him saying, "If thou be the Son of God, come down from the cross" (verse 40). The chief priests were there "mocking him" (verse 41), while the scribes and elders said, "He saved others; himself he cannot save" (verse 42). There, too, were the Roman soldiers who, regarding Him as already dead, gambled for His garments (John 19:23, 24).

But not all who gathered that day were Christ's foes. A few were His friends, though they constituted a pitiably small company. John mentions four. "Now there stood by the cross of Jesus his mother, and his mother's sister, Mary the wife of Cleophas, and Mary Magdalene . . . and the disciple standing by, whom he loved" (John 19:25, 26). Mark adds, "There were also women looking on afar off: among whom was Mary Magdalene, and Mary the mother of James the less and of Joses, and Salome; . . . and many other women which came up with him unto Jerusalem" (Mark 15:40, 41). The men were outnumbered. Jesus had said to His disciples, "All ye shall be offended because of me this night" (Mark 14:27), and then Mark adds, "And they all forsook him, and fled" (Mark 14:50). However, it is most gratifying to know that one of that group of disciples returned to the Saviour's side before He died on the cross. And mark well the fact that our Lord did not rebuke John. He was glad to see the backslider return, especially in that critical hour.

Ever since that day on which Christ suffered and died on the cross, those spectators have had their prototypes. Think of the multiplied millions who attend lenten gatherings, Maundy Thursday and Good Friday services, merely as onlookers and bystanders. They follow the crowds to view the spectacle of Calvary, only to go their merry way to crucify afresh the Son of God and trample under their feet the Saviour's blood.

We must proceed now to focus our attention upon the two in that minority group to whom our Lord addressed Himself. They were His mother Mary, and John. Two translucent thoughts stand out clearly in Christ's words.

A. *The End of a Human Relationship*

Jesus said to Mary, *"Woman, behold thy son!"* Why did He address her in this way? Should He not have called her "mother"? I hesitate to declare dogmatically the reason why, but I am not reluctant at all to venture a guess. No one can question the fact that Christ in His omniscience knew the day was coming when a large segment of Christendom would worship Mary, calling her "The Queen of heaven" and "The Mother of God." Mary was never meant to be worshiped, prayed to, or trusted as the mediatrix for sinners. Nowhere in the Bible is there a trace of the false doctrine that Mary is patroness of the saints. The Word of God is clear. "For there is one God, and one mediator between God and men, the man Christ Jesus" (I Timothy 2:5). Herschel Hobbs says, "One in number, male in sex; Christ Jesus, not Mary."

I must take exception to the explanation which says our Lord was here using the Oriental type of address usually spoken by a man to his mother. Why then did He use a different term when He said to John, "Behold thy mother!" Only the term "mother" could have satisfied Mary's heart in that hour, and yet Jesus did not use it. He is grossly wrong who renders to Mary the veneration, homage and worship due only to Christ.

This was certainly a tense moment for Mary. No doubt memories flashed through her mind — memories of the angel's announcement that she, a virgin, would become a mother;

memories of His birth in Bethlehem where there was no room in the inn; memories of the flight to Egypt when Herod sought the young child's life. But of all the memories in Mary's mind that day, one loomed larger than all the rest. It was the day, after the time of her purification according to the law of Moses, when she brought this Infant to the temple to publicly dedicate Him to God, and heard the aged Simeon prophesy of her, "Yea, a sword shall pierce through thine own soul also" (Luke 2:35). At that very moment at Calvary Simeon's prophecy had been fulfilled, for Mary felt the thrust of the cold steel as it pierced her soul.

Many good and godly mothers have willingly sacrificed their sons for what they believed to be a righteous cause. But of all such noble women, those who have impressed me most deeply are the mothers who dedicated their sons to God, reared them in the nurture and admonition of the Lord, prayed with them and for them, and then continued to make sacrifices in order that a son might serve Christ effectively. As I visit the various mission fields of the world, I will invariably meet a missionary somewhere who has a godly mother back home giving herself to prayer and even financial support so that her boy might be able to take the Gospel to those who have not heard. All such mothers will have their reward. Of course, a sword pierced the soul of many a mother as she bid farewell to her precious son, knowing that she might never see him alive on earth again. But you can be certain that God will not forget these worthy women.

Here Jesus is seen actually breaking the human relationship. At Calvary all human, natural ties were severed. From this point on, Christ will no longer be Mary's *son* but her *Saviour*. He is no longer the son of any human; He is the world's Saviour. The Apostle Paul wrote, "Yea, though we have known Christ after the flesh, yet now henceforth know we him no more" (II Corinthians 5:16). Mary as a sinner did not need the incarnate Christ, but she did need the crucified, resurrected Christ. His Incarnation, apart from His vicarious death, never could have saved Mary, nor us. From Calvary on, believers would be united to Christ by a closer bond than the mere human, physical tie; it was to be for all the redeemed a spiritual relationship.

Our Lord never showed disrespect toward His mother, nor did He elevate her above the rest of humanity. Mary was a sinner by nature as we all are. Neither Mary, nor any other man or woman, save Christ, could possibly be excluded from the divinely-inspired indictment that "There is none righteous, no, not one. . . . For all have sinned, and come short of the glory of God" (Romans 3:10, 23). Mary needed a Saviour, and I believe that she did not merely bear the Son of God who was the Saviour, but that she was born again because she personally trusted Him as her own personal Saviour. Dissolving the human relationship as mother and Son was necessary for the purpose of redemption.

Most of the instances on record which relate to Mary and Jesus have to do with His birth and boyhood. We see her in connection with the annunciation, the journey to Bethlehem, the birth of Christ, the hurried flight to Egypt, the return from Egypt, and the visit to Jerusalem when He was a lad twelve years of age. She appears again at the marriage feast in Cana of Galilee, but when she told Jesus that the guests wanted wine, He said to her, "Woman, what have I to do with thee? mine hour is not yet come" (John 2:4). We may be sure that the Lord is not speaking rudely here. And yet, it is useless to deny that His words were intended to be a rebuke to Mary, for she erred here as on other occasions. Now that He had embarked on His public ministry, there was little in common between Jesus and Mary. I believe that even here He is giving Mary to understand that now that He had officially commenced His Messianic mission, His human relations to her as mother were altered. Her authority over Him had come to an end.

I will not go so far as to say that the Lord resented Mary's suggestion to Him, but none can say He did not make it clear to her that she must not interfere with Him so as to hinder Him from acting in His own way. It is evident that Mary readily agreed to all of this, for she replied, "Whatsoever he saith unto you, do it" (John 2:5). It is true that the birth of Jesus made Mary famous. The angel called her "blessed *among* women" (Luke 1:42), but not "blessed *above* women." Yet it can be well-determined that there did come an end to the human relationship between Jesus and Mary. Mary is set aside, for such human relationships have no place in our Lord's plan of redemption. Of necessity He had to disengage the human ties.

Mary must have understood that this was the end of the human relationship. One other time she is referred to in the New Testament, and there she is taking her place among others who realize their need of prayer (Acts 1:12-14). I believe Schilder is right when he says Mary discovered she had been led from the natural union *with Jesus* to the mystical union *with Christ.*

B. *The Extent of Human Responsibility*

"*Then saith he to the disciple, Behold thy mother!*" (John 19:27). Mary was losing her Son, but Christ gave to her another. He assigned to John the task of carrying on in his phase of His earthly work where He left off. Our Lord was interested in human relationships, and the cross was not to cut off these interests. Thank God He was not the self-centered, self-pitying type of person who can see nothing but his own sufferings and show no sympathy for others. This third word from the cross puts to shame all self-pitying folks who are blind to the mundane needs of others around them. In substance, Jesus is say-ing, "John, I am assigning to you the responsibility of looking out for the well-being of this woman. Be a son to her." That was John's mission.

Did you ever ask yourself why our Lord did not give this assignment to His own brothers and sisters? For one thing, they were not yet believers. Like many others in Nazareth, they re-jected His claims that He was the Messiah. When Jesus said, "A man's foes shall be they of his own household" (Matthew 10:36), He was talking from His own personal experience. Matthew, Mark and Luke, all three, record the incident where His mother and brothers came to see Him, and when one in-formed Him that they desired to see Him, He said, "For who-soever shall do the will of my Father which is in heaven, the same is my brother, and sister, and mother" (Matthew 12:46-50; Mark 3:31-35; Luke 8:19-21). It was not Christ's inten-tion to speak lightly of natural relations, but He knew they were strained in His own household, thus He emphasized the sover-eignty of spiritual relations over the natural. The genuine and abiding relationship is not that of the flesh, but that in the Spirit. As wonderful as earthly relationships are, there is a more intimate relationship between children of God. Our Lord chose to give this assignment to one of God's own rather than to His own brothers and sisters who rejected Him.

There are those in Christendom who deny that Mary had other children in addition to Jesus. But the Bible says, "Is not this the carpenter, the son of Mary, the brother of James, and Joses, and of Juda, and Simon? and are not his sisters here with us? . . . " (Mark 6:3). Here are the names of four brothers and the mention of at least two sisters. To deny that Jesus had brothers or sisters is to deny the plain teaching of Scripture. He had brothers and sisters, but they held an inward grudge against Him. So He said to them, "A prophet is not without honour, but in his own country, and among his own kin, and in his own house" (Mark 6:4, cf. Psalm 69:8). Again He spoke out of His own personal experience. This is why He assigned to John the responsibility of caring for His mother.

In this Jesus set a wonderful example. When God gave the Ten Commandments, He said, "Honour thy father and thy mother" (Exodus 20:12, cf. Ephesians 6:1, 2). Christ fulfilled the Law to the very end. Are you following your Lord's example in the matter of caring for your parents? How do you treat your mother and father? The Bible says, "My son, hear the instruction of thy father, and forsake not the law of thy mother" (Proverbs 1:8). "Hearken unto thy father that begat thee, and despise not thy mother when she is old" (Proverbs 23:22). In His dying hour our Lord magnified the Law. This is the least we can say about Him as He uttered His third word from the cross. Stalker said, "From the pulpit of His cross Jesus preaches to all ages a sermon." May God help each one of us to hear and heed that sermon.

My friends, I am greatly troubled. In our day we are witnessing a growing disregard and disrespect on the part of children and young people for their parents. The example of our Lord is being disregarded and the Scriptures are being disobeyed. True, the Bible does predict that one of the perils in the "last days" shall be that of children being "disobedient to parents" (II Timothy 3:1, 2). But beloved Christian, this condition ought not to exist in the lives of Christ's own. Young people, hear and heed the precepts and practices of the Lord Jesus Christ.

When we see Mary after the Resurrection on her way to Pentecost, we see her other four sons with her (Acts 1:14). They had come to accept Jesus Christ as their Lord and Saviour. Have you?

Chapter 5

CHRIST'S ISOLATION

And about the ninth hour Jesus cried with a loud voice, saying, Eli, Eli, lama sabachthani? that is to say, My God, my God, why hast thou forsaken me?
— Matthew 27:46

A. A PROFOUND MYSTERY

B. A POSITIVE MANIFESTATION

Chapter 5

CHRIST'S ISOLATION

*And about the ninth hour Jesus cried
with a loud voice, saying, Eli, Eli, lama
sabachthani? that is to say, My God,
my God, why hast thou forsaken me?*
— Matthew 27:46

OF THE SEVEN WORDS spoken by our Lord from the cross, this fourth word is the central word in every way. Dr. Samuel Zwemer wrote, "If the cross is the central truth of the New Testament, this cry is the heart of this truth and its deepest expression. This is the Holy of holies to the reverent reader of the Passion."

This fourth saying is different from the other six in that this alone of the seven sayings from the cross is recorded by two of the four gospel writers (Matthew 27:46; Mark 15:34). The first, second and seventh words are recorded by Luke only; the third, fifth and sixth by John only; and the fourth by Matthew and Mark only. Furthermore, in this instance only are our Lord's words as spoken by Him recorded in the original language. He uttered them in either Hebrew or Aramaic. This probably accounts for the misunderstanding on the part of the crowd that stood by the cross. They thought He said Elijah because of the similarity of the sound, and after all it had been prophesied that Elijah would come. Then, too, it is possible that the statement from some of them, "This man calleth for Elias" was meant to be a pun coming from heartless mockers.

I observe two lines of truth in this word. First,

A. *A Profound Mystery*

Of the seven sayings of Christ from the cross, this is no doubt the most difficult to understand and interpret to others. It is reported of Martin Luther that he sat for long hours without food or rest in silent meditation on this fourth word. When he broke the long silence he said, "God forsaken of God! Who can understand that?" Though I cannot endorse fully Luther's conclusion, yet I am not surprised that the text left this impression upon his mind.

Now I do not propose to possess an understanding of this fourth word of our Lord from the cross. Here are depths unfathomable. Here are heights beyond human comprehension. Here is mystery that our finite minds will never probe. I think I can grasp to some extent the meaning of the words, "My God, my God, why hast thou forsaken me?" as they come from the lips of David in Psalm 22:1. But the same words uttered by Christ from the cross baffle me somewhat.

This word has been designated in many ways. It has been called "The Cry of Desolation," "The Cry of Desertion," "The Cry of Dereliction," "The Cry of Despair," "The Cry of Desperation." Try to describe it as you will, but whatever you do, never doubt that Christ spoke it and do not look lightly upon it. This word demands more than a passing glance. It calls for solemn thought and prayerful meditation. We are standing on

holy ground, with our shoes off our feet, for here is an uncon-
sumed bush of Deity.

This fourth word is a prayer. Three of the seven sayings
were prayers addressed to God. The first prayer was the first
word, a prayer of intercession for those who were responsible
for torturing Him. The second was the prayer of this fourth
word, a prayer requesting an explanation for His rejection. The
third prayer was the seventh word, when our Lord calmly and
triumphantly committed His immortal Spirit to the Father. Com-
pare the words in these three prayers,

> *Father,* forgive them; for they know not what
> they do (Luke 23:34).

> My *God,* my *God,* why hast thou forsaken
> me (Matthew 27:46).

> *Father,* into thy hands I commend my spirit
> (Luke 23:46).

Now, what do you see? In the first and third prayers Jesus ad-
dresses God as His *"Father."* But in this instance He says,
"My *God.*" I do not know why the change. Read the prayer
of our Lord in John 17 and you will hear Him say, "Father,"
(verses 1, 5, 21, 24), "Holy Father" (verse 11), "righteous
Father" (verse 25). He frequently referred to the Father as
"God" but only when speaking to others about Him. Christ
stood in that unique relationship of the eternal Son, co-equal
and co-eternal with the Father. When we hear Him for the first
time in the temple as a lad of twelve, He says, "Wist ye not
that I must be about my Father's business?" (Luke 2:49). And
so always and everywhere Christ did so when He addressed Him,
except here. Truly the cross presents strange contrasts. *"Father,*
forgive them." "My *God,* why hast thou forsaken me?" This
is a profound mystery.

Dr. Lockyer writes, "Here it is 'God,' for He appeals to

divine righteousness. Somewhere in the darkness He feels pushed out of the Father's heart in a desolate forest. Yet He clings to divine righteousness. In spite of the mystery of the moment He knew that God as God must be doing right."

There is mystery in the fact that this is the only time, as far as I have knowledge, that Jesus ever asked the Father a question. During His earthly ministry He always accepted the Father's will without question. Never once did He so much as ask why, when, where or how. He only could say, "I do always those things that please him" (John 8:29). Here, I say again, is profound mystery.

There was the mystery of the darkness. "Now from the sixth hour there was darkness over all the land unto the ninth hour" (Matthew 27:45). I maintain that this darkness was closely related to the fourth word. Something was happening in that darkness that none of the redeemed will ever know. It was at the close of the period of darkness, at three o'clock in the afternoon, that Christ uttered this cry of dereliction. For three hours He was in the light; for three hours He was in the darkness. This was not a natural eclipse as some would tell us. It could have been, for it was the time of the Feast which means that the moon was full. This darkness was supernatural, made so by God.

Here is a strange paradox! Christ "the Light of the world" (John 8:12), "the true Light, which lighteth every man that cometh into the world" (John 1:9), is suspended in the darkness between heaven and earth. Christ's words and the darkness from which He uttered them, are of deepest mystery. God left His Son in darkness but He never left His people in darkness. "And the Lord said unto Moses, Stretch out thine hand toward heaven, that there may be darkness over the land of Egypt, even darkness which may be felt. And Moses stretched forth his hand toward heaven; and there was a thick darkness in all the land of Egypt three days: They saw not one another, neither rose any from his place for three days: but all the children of Israel had light in their dwellings" (Exodus 10:21-23).

But at Calvary, God's beloved Son, in whom He was well-pleased, hung in supernatural darkness, a million times darker than the ninth plague that befell Egypt, and that was a darkness which could be felt. He saved Israel from Egypt's dark judgment, but His Holy Son He permitted to pass through the outer darkness. I say again, here is a profound mystery.

B. *A Positive Manifestation*

Not all that is attached to this fourth word is mystery. This utterance of unequalled secrecy is likewise one of fullest manifestation. It was a manifestation of Christ's thoughts about the Old Testament Scriptures. The words He spoke are found verbatim in the Psalter. David wrote by inspiration, "My God, my God, why hast thou forsaken me?" (Psalm 22:1). This psalm is the first of a trilogy dealing with the two advents of Christ and His present intercessory ministry in behalf of His own. We see *The Saviour's Cross* (Psalm 22), *The Shepherd's Crook* (Psalm 23) and *The Sovereign's Crown* (Psalm 24). Now this twenty-second Psalm may have a primary association in David's life during the period of Saul's persecution of David. We know that David wrote this psalm (Acts 2:29-31). But its language reaches far beyond David's suffering to the atoning sufferings of Christ. Read the entire psalm carefully and you will see that the Sufferer is your Saviour.

Dr. Scroggie points out some parallels between Psalm 22 and our Lord's death: Christ's dying cry (verse 1); the mockers gathered around the cross, and their taunts (verses 7, 8, 12, 13); torture by crucifixion (verse 16); the distorted body (verses 14, 17); the parched tongue and lips (verse 15); the divided garments and unrent vesture (verse 18); and at last the sudden silence in death.

But why is there no mention of the spear thrust? Because Christ was already dead when that was done, and the Sufferer is not represented as telling what happened after He had died. This psalm is a vivid description of Christ's sufferings on the cross. The facts fit the case perfectly. Here, then, is a pure prophecy substantiated by our Lord's dying words. There is no mystery here, only a positive manifestation that the Bible is the inspired Word of God.

This cry was a manifestation of God's attitude toward sin. It is a known fact that God hates and judges sin. A minor prophet with a major message wrote that God is "of purer eyes than to behold evil, and canst not look on iniquity" (Habakkuk 1:13). Whatever else I am not certain of, I am certain that God detests evil and cannot look upon it. All wickedness is utterly abhorrent to Him because of His holiness. God and evil are opposites. "God is light, and in him is no darkness at all" (I John 1:5). Darkness is everywhere in Scripture symbolic of evil. Jesus said, "Men loved darkness rather than light, because their deeds were evil" (John 3:19).

Now we know that the very evil that God hated and could not look upon was, in that dark hour, upon the Lord Jesus. The death of Christ was a substitutionary death for all sin and for all sinners, so that actually there was placed on Christ "the iniquity of us all" (Isaiah 53:6). He was "the Lamb of God, which taketh away the sin of the world" (John 1:29).

On the Day of Atonement two goats were to be taken and presented before the Lord. One of these goats was called the scapegoat. "And Aaron shall lay both his hands upon the head of the live goat, and confess over him all the iniquities of the children of Israel, and all their transgressions in all their sins, putting them upon the head of the goat, and shall send him away by the hand of a fit man into the wilderness. And the goat shall bear upon him all their iniquities unto a land not inhabited: and he shall let go the goat in the wilderness" (Leviticus 16:21, 22). The scapegoat is introduced after the first goat had been killed, and since the scapegoat represents Christ, it suggests the effects or results of the atonement. The scapegoat bore *"all the iniquities"* as it was sent off into the wilderness, the place of forgiveness and forgetfulness. Thus, in His dying our Lord Jesus Christ was bearing in His body all the sins of the human race. "Who his own self bare our sins in his own body on the tree" (I Peter 2: 24).

One of the peculiar doctrines of the Seventh-day Adventists is their unscriptural view of the *atonement.* It is here where their deceptive doctrine of demons deviates most from the teaching of Scripture. While Seventh-day Adventism claims to base its beliefs upon the Bible as the Word of God, one needs only to examine the writings of William Miller and Ellen G. Harmon White to see for himself how far adrift they are from what the Bible teaches.

On the doctrine of the *atonement,* the sect of Seventh-day Adventism has its own point of belief which is its private property. They agree that on the Day of Atonement a scapegoat was burdened with the sins of the people and then sent into the wilderness. But to them the scapegoat does not typify Christ. Mrs. White says that it is Satan, the author of sin, "upon whom the sins of the truly penitent will finally be placed." Nothing is farther from the truth. The darkness at Calvary was shutting out from view the sinless Son of God bearing in His own body the sins of the world.

Because of the heinousness of sin and the absolute holiness of God, the darkness was necessary to Him. The awful doom of sinners is to be punished with everlasting destruction "from the presence of the Lord" (II Thessalonians 1:9). But in that dark hour at Calvary Christ was shut off from His Father's presence. The reason is clear. The psalm of prophecy gives the answer, "Thou art holy" (Psalm 22:3). Sin excludes from God's presence. God's holy character could not do less than judge sin even though that sin be upon Christ Himself.

The fourth word is a manifestation of the basis of our salvation. The Bible says, "For he hath made him to be sin for us, who knew no sin; that we might be made the righteousness of God in him" (II Corinthians 5:21). The cross was the way of substitution, and the Son of God Himself was chosen to be the Substitute. Christ so completely took the sinner's place that, in order to redeem men from the curse of the Law, He became a curse for all (Galatians 3:13). The holy, sinless One bore all the sins of all sinners since Adam. Think upon this if you can! Meditate long and hard on it! In order to pay the price for the trillions of sins committed by billions of people during the six thousand or more years of human history, He had to bear the full penalty. That meant separation from God the Father; it meant the awful pangs of hell.

Because He was so utterly identified with sin and sinners, He was banished from God's presence. He descended into hell. He fought the powers of darkness and death in their own element. And had He not gone all the way in bearing our judgment, what He suffered in that dark hour would not have atoned for us, but instead it would have meant the endless doom of every one of us. Though sin was utterly foreign to Him, thank God He voluntarily became the representative Sin-Bearer for the whole race of mankind.

Why did He utter this cry? Simply that we might not have to utter it. He was treading the winepress of the fierceness of God's wrath alone. Three times Christ warned men of the "outer darkness" (Matthew 8:12; 22:13; 25:30). But He did more than merely warn them. He voluntarily plunged into the outer darkness so that you and I never need to suffer its bitter pangs. It was not possible to transfer our sin without transferring its penalty. The Substitute for sinners must be rejected as a sinner. Sin, in its finality, is to forsake God; sin, in its final dealings with man, is to be God-forsaken. But, praise God, it has been transferred, and He was forsaken that we might be made free and forgiven. There is no longer any mystery as to the basis of our salvation. There never was such a darkness at noon before, and there never will be for you if you come to Christ and trust Him at once. God will never forsake you if you trust His Son whom He forsook for you.

There is no mystery as to Christ's faith in that dark hour. This cry was not occasioned by unbelief. Some professing Christians I have met talk about God having forsaken them in their trial, but this is merely an excuse for their coldness of heart and lack of faith. It is our unbelief that makes us talk about God forgetting and forsaking us. But our Lord was a stranger to unbelief. The man whose faith is weak may talk about God, but the believing one will say, "*My* God." In Christ's darkest hour the Father was His own God. This suggests to me a victorious faith. Can faith cling to God in the dark? It most certainly can. But if faith fizzles out in the dark, it is not the faith of our Lord Jesus Christ.

There is no virtue in being discouraged and defeated. Begging sympathy from your friends will add nothing to your already weakened faith. Carry your burden to God. Cast your care upon Him. Surround your trial with a faith that will not surrender. Let your "whys" be in confidence and trust in the living God who doeth all things well. Let every cry to God be a faith-cry, not a cry *against* God. Christ knew that the Father was for Him and not against Him, therefore He will not shrink from the trial. It is never wrong to enquire about unanswered questions as long as we do so in faith.

It was on this very question of Christ's faith that His enemies attacked Him. They said, "He trusted in God; let him deliver him now, if he will have him: for he said, I am the Son of God" (Matthew 27:43). Though there was no apparent deliverance at that moment, the Saviour continued trusting. A faith that does not rest upon God in deepest trial and darkest times is not the victorious faith of a true child of God. The faith that saves is the faith that sustains, and in the long run such faith will silence the enemy.

Chapter 6

THE FIFTH WORD

CHRIST'S IDENTIFICATION

I thirst. — John 19:28

A. THE CRY OF THE HUMAN ONE

B. THE CRY OF THE HOLY ONE

Chapter 6

THE FIFTH WORD

CHRIST'S IDENTIFICATION

I thirst. — John 19:28

THIS FIFTH WORD of Christ from the cross differs from the six other words in that it is the only word in which attention is drawn to Himself in His suffering and agony. His first words were definitely in the interest of others — *"Father, forgive them; for they know not what they do"*; *"To day shalt thou be with me in paradise"*; *"Woman, behold thy son!"* While the fourth word spoke of His being forsaken of the Father, it did not bear directly upon His physical suffering as does this fifth word: *"I thirst."*

This probably was the moment of our Lord's severest physical distress. There was the agony in the garden, those harrowing hearings before Caiaphas and Annas, the public mock trials in the court of Pilate and Herod, the scourging with the Roman leather whip, the crown of thorns pressed upon His head, the load of the heavy cross, the piercing of the nails through His flesh, the rays of the hot sun at one hour and the awful darkness in the next.

But of all the physical agonies that come to the human body, thirst is terrible beyond the power of words to describe. One writer seems to minimize the force of Christ's words by saying, "He only revealed a condition." That may be so, but at the same time it was the only such condition He ever revealed. Not once did He speak out against His tormentors or utter a complaint about His physical sufferings. But the pangs of thirst were more than He could bear.

Before we attempt to speak further about this fifth utterance of our Lord, let us look at the entire text which forms its setting. John writes: "After this, Jesus knowing that all things were now accomplished, that the scripture might be fulfilled, saith, I thirst" (John 19:28). Yes, the Scripture was fulfilled, for even this small detail had been prophesied. Listen to the words of the psalmist as he speaks prophetically the words of Christ, penned one thousand years before His crucifixion, "They gave me also gall for my meat; and in my thirst they gave me vinegar to drink" (Psalm 69:21). This is only one of many prophecies of our Lord's last days on earth which were fulfilled and which prove that the Bible is the inerrant Word of God.

Arthur W. Pink said, "How marvellously complete was the prophetic foreview! No essential item was missing from it. Every important detail of the great Tragedy had been written down beforehand. The betrayal by a familiar friend (Psalm 41:9), the forsaking of the disciples through being offended at him (Psalm 31:11), the fake accusation (Psalm 35:11), the silence before His judges (Isaiah 53:7), the being crucified (Psalm 22:16), the mockery of the spectators (Psalm 109:25), the taunt of non-deliverance (Psalm 22:7, 8), the gambling for His garments (Psalm 22:18), the prayer for His enemies (Isaiah 53:12), the being forsaken of God (Psalm 22:1), the thirsting (Psalm 69:21), the yielding of His spirit into the hands of the Father (Psalm 31:5), the bones not broken (Psalm 34:20), the burial in a rich man's tomb (Isaiah 53:9) — all plainly foretold centuries before they came to pass. What convincing evidence for the divine inspiration of the Scriptures! "How firm a foundation, ye saints of the Lord, is laid for your faith in His excellent Word!"

And now, returning to the cry of our Lord, I see at least two thoughts on which we might ponder. These I have called, *The Cry of the Human One* and *The Cry of the Holy One*. First,

A. The Cry of the Human One

Most students of the Bible recognize in this word an expression of Christ's human nature. Here we see His complete humanity, His identification with the human race. The Bible is clear in its teaching of the absolute Deity of our Lord Jesus Christ, that He is "very God of very God." But the Scriptures are equally clear in setting forth the humanity of Christ, that He is "very man of very man." The Word declares, "And without controversy great is the mystery of godliness: God was manifest in the flesh . . ." (I Timothy 3:16). The fusion of Deity and humanity in the Virgin's womb is not a fit subject for the speculations or debates of the unregenerate man, for "the natural man receiveth not the things of the Spirit of God: for they are foolishness unto him: neither can he know them, because they are spiritually discerned" (I Corinthians 2:14). The reasoning of the unregenerate mind leads to the speculative and philosophic conclusion that "Jesus of Nazareth was merely a man possessing a spark of divinity," or, as another has crudely stated it, "Here is a man who was a humanized God." But both are wrong! Christ is the God-man, forever God, and now forever Man. When Jesus was born into the world, the eternal Word became flesh and dwelt among men (John 1:1, 14).

"Who is the Redeemer of God's elect?" In answer to this question, the Shorter Catechism says, "The only Redeemer of God's elect is the Lord Jesus Christ, who, being the eternal Son of God, became man, and so was, and continueth to be God, and man, in two distinct natures, and one Person forever." Christ the eternal Son of God became man by taking to Himself a human body (Hebrews 10:5). His body was conceived by the power of the Holy Spirit (Luke 1:35). While Christ was (and is) God in the fullest sense, He was (and is) also perfect humanity. He was the Seed of the woman (Genesis 3:15, cf. Galatians 4:4), a truly human person who knew the reactions and experiences which are common to human nature. There were times when He was hungry (Matthew 4:2; 21:18), weary (John 4:6), angry (Mark 3:5), compassionate (Matthew 9:36; Mark 1:41), joyful (John 15:11), sorrowful (Matthew 26:37), tempted (Matthew 4:1; Hebrews 4:15), and as we see Him in our text, thirsty (John 19:28, cf. John 4:6, 7). He called Himself a "man" (John 8:40), and He was called a "man" by Pilate (John 19:5), Peter (Acts 2:22), Paul (I Timothy 2:5) and others. Christ "was made in the likeness of men" (Philippians 2:7) because "it behoved him to be made like unto his brethren" (Hebrews 2:17).

We would not argue the point that this fifth word of Christ from the cross evidenced His humanity. Thirst is natural to all *men* everywhere. God the Father does not thirst in heaven. Angels do not thirst. Nor shall believers thirst in their glorified bodies, for "they shall hunger no more, neither thirst any more" (Revelation 7:16). But our Lord thirsted while He was here on earth. At Jacob's well He requested of the Samaritan woman: "Give me to drink" (John 4:7). But when the death-dew was on His brow, His extreme agony and suffering brought on a burning feverishness with its accompanying unbearable dryness in His throat, mouth and stomach. The extremity of His thirst is described by the psalmist in the words "My tongue cleaveth to my jaws" (Psalm 22:15), "My throat is dried" (Psalm 69:3). It is possible that any of us may yet know a measure of such thirst in our dying moments. I trust not! But until now we have known nothing of it.

Once again, as I think of Christ's thirst on the cross, I see the awful pangs of One passing through the hot flames of hell. This thirst was an indication of our Lord's suffering substitution for sinners. In His death He hung in the sinner's stead, and He must therefore pay the penalty for the sinner's sins. In our Lord's fourth word, "My God, my God, why hast thou forsaken me?" we see the anguish of His soul. Here in His fifth word, "I thirst," we see the torture of His body. Both forms of torture await the unbeliever in hell. The bodies of the wicked dead shall be raised so that both body and soul will be in torment forever. The rich man in Hades, being in torment, cried and said, "Have mercy on me, and send Lazarus, that he may dip the tip of his finger in water, and cool my tongue; for I am tormented in this flame" (Luke 16:24). Please do not think me irreverent for comparing the thirst of the sinless Saviour with that of the unbelieving rich man who was a child of hell. But I submit for your serious thinking that, in order to pay the debt of man's sin, Jesus Christ, in that moment of God-forsakenness, passed through the fires of judgment. The Substitute must experience the full judgment of those in whose place He stands. Had He not done so, there could be no escape for any of us.

Thank God that Jesus thirsted. Had He not thirsted, every one of us would have thirsted forever in hell, and like the rich man in hell, all who choose to go there will learn that between hell and heaven there is a great gulf fixed, so that they who would pass from the one to the other cannot (Luke 16:26). But He who thirsted and died on Calvary's cross, rose again from death and the grave. He offers to all who will receive from Him the water of life. He said, "Whosoever drinketh of the water that I shall give him shall never thirst; but the water that I shall give him shall be in him a well of water springing up into everlasting life" (John 4:14). "And the Spirit and the bride say, Come. And let him that heareth say, Come. And let him that is athirst come. And whosoever will, let him take the water of life freely" (Revelation 22:17).

The world rushes hither and yon in its mad pursuit to fill the aching void in man's soul. Men and women hasten from one thing to another in an attempt to quench the soul's thirst. They go from one night club to another, from one brand of cigarette to another, from one kind of alcoholic beverage to another, from one sport to another, and even from one partner in sex to another. But with it all, the heart remains unsatisfied until Christ is received by faith. He made us and He alone can quench our thirst and satisfy us. Oh, thirsty one, come at once to the Saviour and drink deeply of the water of life.

And now I see in this fifth word,

B. *The Cry of the Holy One*

When our Lord said, "I thirst," there was more involved in this word than His mere physical thirst. We miss the full meaning of what He said if we interpret His desire to be totally devoid of spiritual content. In His humanity He did crave refreshment for His body, but as the Holy One He has a deep spiritual thirst for the souls of men. This cry of our Lord reveals a strange mixture of the human and the divine. Remember, on the cross He was the God-Man, and never did He lay aside His Deity.

The purpose of Christ's Incarnation was that He might rescue sinners from hell. He said, "Even as the Son of man came not to be ministered unto, but to minister, and to give his life a ransom for many" (Matthew 20:28). "I came . . . to call

. . . sinners to repentance" (Mark 2:17). "For the Son of man is come to seek and to save that which was lost" (Luke 19:10). His whole life was one glorious movement in which He sought to save men. He was concerned about our spiritual welfare. "And Jesus, when he came out, saw much people, and was moved with compassion toward them, because they were as sheep not having a shepherd: and he began to teach them many things" (Mark 6:34). And so He moved steadily on to the cross ever reaching out in holy compassion to save poor, lost sinners, and the cross was His final demonstration on earth of that compassion. His first two words were words of compassion: "Father, forgive them for they know not what they do" (Luke 23:34), and then to the dying thief as He said, "To day shalt thou be with me in paradise" (Luke 23:43). Never has there been a more magnificent display of concern and compassion for the welfare of others.

Some unbelieving critics of our Lord have concluded that He must be *either* divine or human. But they only create for themselves an irreconcilable dilemma when they refuse to believe that He was *both* divine and human. A merely human Jesus could not have died as did our Lord. Until the very end He was reaching out with compassion to save the lost. On the cross we can see clearly the relation of the two natures in Christ. In His composite personality the two natures of Christ are so united that it is perfectly correct to say that Jesus thirsted and God thirsted. The Holy Spirit reminds us that Christ's enemies did not crucify merely a man, but "the Lord of Glory" (I Corinthians 2:8). The thirst of Deity is that age-long desire in the heart of God to bring men to Himself, and Calvary is the full and final exhibition of His holy compassion.

Consider once more Christ's meeting with the woman at the well. True, He asked for a drink of water and He needed that drink of water. But if He craved a drink of cooling water from those human hands, He craved with a greater desire the salvation of that woman's soul. Hear Him as He speaks to her, "If thou knewest the gift of God, and who it is that saith to thee, Give me to drink; thou wouldest have asked of him, and he would have given thee living water" (John 4:10). Yes, He stopped at that well for a drink of water, but it was also that He might give to the woman the water of life. He thirsted to deliver her from the thirst of hell.

There is even now in the heart of our Lord, as there always has been, a thirst for souls, a thirst for your soul. He must come again to judge the world, as He promised, but presently He is "longsuffering to us-ward, not willing that any should perish, but that all should come to repentance" (II Peter 3:9). He thirsts to save you, to bless you and to have communion with you. He sees your emptiness and offers you His fullness. He sees your doom and offers to deliver you. He loves you and wants to save you. This is the thirst of the Holy One. And that thirst of His will never be satisfied until there is a response in your heart to His love for you.

Behold His heart of tender compassion as He thirsts for Peter's love! "Simon, son of Jonas, lovest thou me more than these? . . . Simon, son of Jonas, lovest thou me? . . . Simon, son of Jonas, lovest thou me?" (John 21:15-17). What pleading! What thirst! Three times His compassionate thirsty heart reaches out to draw Peter to Himself.

Even now the thirsty One stands at the door of your heart, and says, "Behold, I stand at the door, and knock: if any man hear my voice, and open the door, I will come in to him, and sup with him, and he with me" (Revelation 3:20). Oh, that we might thirst after Him and receive Him! The psalmist said, "As the hart panteth after the water brooks, so panteth my soul after Thee, O God. My soul thirsteth for God, for the living God" (Psalm 42:1,2). "O God, thou art my God; early will I seek thee; my soul thirsteth for thee, my flesh longeth for thee in a dry and thirsty land, where no water is" (Psalm 63:1). Jesus said, "Blessed are they which do hunger and thirst after righteousness: for they shall be filled" (Matthew 5:6); and "he that believeth on me shall never thirst" (John 6:35). "If any man thirst, let him come unto me, and drink" (John 7:37). He thirsts for you. Will you come to Him?

Chapter 7

CHRIST'S INDEMNITY

It is finished. — John 19:30

A. THE CONSUMMATION OF PROPHETIC SCRIPTURES

B. THE CULMINATION OF PERSONAL SUFFERINGS

C. THE COMPLETION OF A PERFECT SACRIFICE

D. THE CONQUEST OVER THE POWER OF SATAN

Chapter 7

CHRIST'S INDEMNITY

It is finished. — John 19:30

THOSE WHO TEACH us Greek keep reminding us that the ancient Greeks were aware of their ability to say much in a few words. They could put "a sea of matter in a drop of language." They had a motto, "Much in little." Or as my dear friend, the late Dr. Arthur Whiting, has noted, the Latin would say, *Multum in parvo.* The Greek who could say a great deal with little language was credited with having reached the peak of oratory.

Both the fifth and sixth words of Christ from the cross appear in just one exclamatory term in the Greek New Testament. The fifth saying, *"I thirst,"* is not in two words as it appears here in the King James Version, but one (Greek, *dipso*). Nor is the sixth saying of our Lord in three words as it appears in our English text, *"It is finished,"* but one (Greek, *tetelestai*), meaning "finished." In this one word "finished" there is a divine declaration so glorious that, ever since Jesus spoke it, the devil has kept busy trying to hide its real meaning from the human race. This is Christ's word of victory, His great oratorio of triumph. This word embraces the other six words, and much more.

I believe I have some idea why the translators put the one Greek word into three English words. Had they left it in the original, we might be following one or another of the satanic delusions which have deceived so many. We might be in a quandary asking ourselves, "Who was finished," and then end up with the devil's dream that He (Christ) is finished. I do not believe my imagination is running away with me when I tell you that many of His enemies who watched Him die said to themselves, and possibly to each other, "Ah, He admits He is finished." But mark well one striking difference between the fifth and sixth words. That difference is between the words "I" and "it." In the previous word He said, "*I* thirst," calling attention to His *Person.* In this sixth word He said, "*It* is finished," calling attention to His *work.* Here it is not the "I" but the "it." Our Lord did not say, "I am finished." He said, "It is finished."

And now may the Holy Spirit bless our hearts as we pursue our study of "it," the finished work of Christ at Calvary. Just what did Christ have in His mind when He spoke this sixth word? What was it He finished when He cried, "Tetelestai"? I see at least four possibilities.

A. *The Consummation of Prophetic Scriptures*

Here we see Old Testament prophecies brought to their full and final development. When He said, "*It is finished*" He meant that every prophecy concerning Him, up to His last conscious moments before His death, had been fulfilled.

John writes, "After this, Jesus knowing that all things were now accomplished, *that the scripture might be fulfilled*, saith, I thirst. Now there was set a vessel full of vinegar (or sour wine): and they filled a spunge with vinegar, and put it upon hyssop, and put it to his mouth. When Jesus therefore had received the vinegar, he said, "It is finished" (John 19:28-30). The Lord Jesus, hanging on the cross in full possession of all His mental faculties, having refused the stupefying drink offered to Him previously (Matthew 27:34), knew that the many prophecies concerning His first coming had been fulfilled except this final one. When He said, "I thirst," not one single prophecy had failed. It was not that He was thirsty only, but that "the scripture might be fulfilled." When Jesus therefore had received the vinegar, He said, "It is finished."

It is true that there still remained prophecies to be fulfilled, such as (1) the passing of His spirit into the hands of the Father (Psalm 31:5), (2) the piercing of His body with the spear (Zechariah 12:10), (3) the preserving of His bones unbroken (Psalm 34:20), and (4) the placing of His body in the rich man's grave (Isaiah 53:9). But there remained nothing more for the Saviour to finish.

The prophecies which had to do with His first advent, all of them, had now been actually fulfilled. He was the woman's Seed (Genesis 3:15, cf. Galatians 4:4); born of a Virgin (Isaiah 7:14, cf. Matthew 1:18); in Bethlehem of Judea (Micah 5:2, cf. Matthew 2:6; John 7:42); of the seed of Abraham (Genesis 22:18 cf. Matthew 1:1); of the lineage of David (II Samuel 7: 12, 13, cf. Romans 1:3). He was named before He was born (Isaiah 49:1, cf. Matthew 1:21; Luke 1:30, 31). He was a descendant of the Tribe of Judah (Genesis 49:10, cf. Revelation 5:5). These are but a few of the many prophecies concerning Him which were fulfilled at His first Advent, not to mention those relating to His sufferings and death. They were all "finished," fulfilled, or "accomplished," as the same Greek word *Tetelestai* is translated in John 19:28. He could say, "I have finished the work which thou gavest me to do" (John 17:4).

Charles Haddon Spurgeon, in his own masterful and majestic way, stated it as follows, "There is not a single jewel of promise, from that first emerald which fell on the threshold of Eden, to that last sapphire-stone of Malachi, which was not set in the breast-plate of the true High Priest. Nay, there is not a type, from the red heifer downward to the turtle-dove, from the hyssop upwards to Solomon's temple itself, which was not fulfilled in Him; and not a prophecy, whether spoken on Chebar's bank, or on the shores of Jordan; not a dream of wise men, whether they had received it in Babylon, or in Samaria, or in Judea, which was not now fully wrought out in Christ Jesus.

"What a wonderful thing it is, that a mass of promises, and prophecies, and types, apparently so heterogeneous, should all be accomplished in one Person! Take away Christ for one moment, and I will give the Old Testament to any wise man living, and say to him, 'Take this; this is a problem; go home and construct in your imagination an ideal character who shall exactly fit all that which is herein foreshadowed; remember, he must be a prophet like unto Moses, and yet a champion like Joshua; he must be an Aaron and a Melchisedek; he must be both David and Solomon, Noah and Jonah, Judah and Joseph. Nay, he must not only be the lamb that was slain, and the scape-goat that was not slain, the turtle-dove that was dipped in blood, and the priest who slew the bird, but he must be the altar, the tabernacle, the mercy seat, and the shewbread.' Nay, to puzzle this wise man further, we remind him of prophecies so apparently contradictory, that one would think they never could meet in one man." Praise be to God they all did meet in one Man. That Man is our Saviour and God. "It is finished."

In the second place, I see in this word of Christ from the cross,

B. *The Culmination of His Personal Sufferings*

One hesitates to attempt to depict the sufferings of our Lord. We know so little of suffering ourselves. We can only go to the divine records and there glean what the Holy Spirit was pleased to write. We do know that our Lord's suffering was not confined to physical pain. There was the unutterable sorrow and anguish of both His spirit and mind. At Gethsemane He said to Peter, James and John, "My soul is exceeding sorrowful, even unto death" (Matthew 26:38). This sorrow was a part of His suffering.

But He did suffer physically. He was holy, spotless and undefiled, showing love and kindness to all men wherever He went. And yet He was misunderstood, criticized, threatened, beaten, spit upon, slapped, tortured, abused and finally condemned to die the shameful, ignominious death of a criminal on a cross.

Listen as the Scriptures speak of His sufferings. "I gave my back to the smiters, and my cheeks to them that plucked off the hair: I hid not my face from shame and spitting" (Isaiah 50:6). "All they that see me laugh me to scorn . . . they gaped upon me with their mouths . . . the assembly of the wicked have inclosed me: they pierced my hands and my feet" (Psalm 22:7, 13, 16). "I looked for some to take pity, but there was none; and for comforters, but I found none. They gave me also gall for my meat; and in my thirst they gave me vinegar to drink" (Psalm 69:20, 21).

Listen again as the Holy Spirit depicts our Lord's sufferings through the pen of Isaiah the prophet — "He is despised and rejected of men; a man of sorrows, and acquainted with grief: and we hid as it were our faces from him; he was despised, and we esteemed him not. Surely he hath borne our griefs, and carried our sorrows: yet we did esteem him stricken, smitten of God, and afflicted. But he was wounded for our transgressions, he was bruised for our iniquities: the chastisement of our peace was upon him; and with his stripes we are healed. All we like sheep have gone astray; we have turned every one to his own way; and the LORD hath laid on him the iniquity of us all. He was oppressed, and he was afflicted, yet he opened not his mouth:

he is brought as a lamb to the slaughter, and as a sheep before her shearers is dumb, so he openeth not his mouth. He was taken from prison and from judgment: and who shall declare his generation? for he was cut off out of the land of the living: for the transgression of my people was he stricken. And he made his grave with the wicked, and with the rich in his death; because he had done no violence, neither was any deceit in his mouth. Yet it pleased the LORD to bruise him . . ." (Isaiah 53:3-10).

The sufferings of Christ were voluntary. He knew from the beginning what would befall Him. The idea of Christ's death being that of a martyr is nowhere to be found in Scripture. His own testimony of His forthcoming death was one of expectation. Hear Him say, "From that time forth began Jesus to shew unto his disciples, how that he must go unto Jerusalem, and suffer many things of the elders and chief priests and scribes, and be killed, and be raised again the third day" (Matthew 16:21). "Likewise shall also the Son of man suffer" (Matthew 17:12). "With desire I have desired to eat this passover with you before I suffer" (Luke 22:15). "Then he said unto them, O fools, and slow of heart to believe all that the prophets have spoken: Ought not Christ to have suffered these things?" (Luke 24:25, 26). "I am the good shepherd: the good shepherd giveth his life for the sheep" (John 10:11). "Therefore doth my Father love me, because I lay down my life, that I might take it again. No man taketh it from me, but I lay it down of myself. I have power to lay it down, and I have power to take it again. This commandment have I received of my Father" (John 10:17, 18). He faced the sufferings of His life and death knowingly and willingly, but praise be to God, His sufferings are finished forever.

In the third place, I see in this word of Christ from the cross,

C. *The Completion of a Perfect Sacrifice*

The idea of a sacrifice for sins is found throughout the entire Word of God, telling us that a blood sacrifice has always been associated with the sins of the human race. From those coats of skins which provided a covering for Adam and Eve (Genesis 3:21), to Abel's lamb (Genesis 4:4, cf. Hebrews 11:4), to Noah's sacrifices (Genesis 8:20), to Abraham's lamb provided by God Himself (Genesis 22:7-13), to those slain lambs in Jewish homes on the night of the passover (Exodus 12), to the bloody sacrifices offered by Aaron, the high priests and the Levites every morning and every evening (Leviticus 1-7), to the river of blood which flowed endlessly from Solomon's temple and on through six thousand years of human history, tell us that "without shedding of blood is no remission" (Hebrews 9:22).

When God gave instructions to Moses for the building of the tabernacle in the wilderness, He made provision for every utensil and piece of furniture. But there was no provision for a chair. There was the altar, the laver, the table, the lamp, the curtain, the veil, the lampstand. But there was no chair, no place to sit down. There was never an end to the work necessary for the atonement of sins. It was sacrifice, sacrifice, sacrifice year in and year out until the people might have cried, "Will the sacrifices never be finished? Must we always have before us a remembrance of sin?"

Then one day the world's Redeemer came. The Great High Priest appeared to make one final sacrifice for sin, thereby putting to an end the need for further sacrifices. He offered Himself as the one perfect Sacrifice. And in His dying moments something happened that was unique and supernatural. "The veil of the temple was rent in twain from the top to the bottom" (Matthew 27:51). Why did God do this? I'll tell you why. The veil which hung between the two compartments of the tabernacle before the Holy of Holies, into which the Jewish high priest went every year, was rent by God Himself so that no more sacrifice would be necessary, and never again would it be necessary to sprinkle blood upon the Mercy Seat.

But this is not all. The story does not end here. The Man who died on that cross was buried in a grave; on the third day He arose again and ascended into heaven and did something no other high priest did before Him. He *sat down!* Here it is stated clearly in the records of God. "And every priest (Old Testament priest) *standeth daily* ministering and offering oftentimes the same sacrifices, which can never take away sins: But this man, after he had offered one sacrifice for sins for ever, *sat down* on the right hand of God" (Hebrews 10:11, 12). "For by one offering he hath perfected for ever them that are sanctified" (Hebrews 10:14). Here, unsaved ones, is the best news you ever heard. Christ, by His death at Calvary, has paid the debt in full for your sins. In fact, the debt is so completely wiped out that there is nothing more to pay. Jesus paid it all. The fact that He *sat down* indicates that God was forever satisfied with the Perfect Sacrifice. Christ "put away sin by the sacrifice of himself" (Hebrews 9:26). Yes, He "endured the cross, despising the shame, and is *set down* at the right hand of the throne of God" (Hebrews 12:2). Trust Him and rejoice! "It is finished."

In the fourth place, I see in this word of Christ from the cross,

D. *The Conquest Over the Power of Satan*

By His death on the cross our Lord conquered death. He brought to nought this last dread enemy. The cross was the final overthrow of Satan's strange power over the bodies of men. Until Calvary Satan held the keys of death. God had said to our first parents, "In the day that thou eatest thereof thou shalt surely die" (Genesis 2:17). But when Satan appeared, he said to Eve, "Ye shall not surely die" (Genesis 3:4). Satan's words were a lie. He knew what God had said, and he knew furthermore that God would carry out His warning. This was exactly what the devil wanted to happen, and it is precisely what did happen.

When our first parents chose to die they did so by turning themselves over to Satan. Now keep in mind the fact that it was God who pronounced the death sentence because of sin, thus the devil has demanded death on the authority of God's own word. He knows that until sin is done away, he can claim man's death. "Wherefore, as by one man sin entered into the world, and death by sin; and so death passed upon all men, for that all have sinned" (Romans 5:12). "For the wages of sin is death . . ." (Romans 6:23). As long as the sin barrier remained, Satan held the keys of death. Thus he holds the sinner in the power of death until God officially releases him. And the cross is the place where the legal release is given.

This is all explained more clearly in the epistle to the Hebrews. "Forasmuch then as the children are partakers of flesh and blood, he also himself likewise took part of the same; that through death he might destroy him that had the power of death, that is, the devil" (Hebrews 2:14). This verse is telling us that Christ became one with us in our humanity that He might enter into our death, endure the penalty of our sins, thereby satisfying the demands of God and releasing us from death.

The Law of God demanded and still does demand death for sin. "The soul that sinneth, it shall die" (Ezekiel 18:4). Satan is therefore justified in demanding the death penalty for all sinners. But God in His love and mercy and grace found a way to save sinners. That way was through the death of His Son who took upon Himself flesh and blood, yet without sin, and paid the full penalty.

But He did not remain dead. By His Resurrection He gives new life and guarantees that our mortal and corruptible bodies will one day put on immortality and incorruptibility. Death has lost its sting and the grave is no longer victor (I Corinthians 15:53-57). It was with this end in view that the Son of God became incarnate.

In this respect the Apostle Paul says that Christ, "having spoiled principalities and powers, he made a shew of them openly, triumphing over them in it" (that is, in the cross) (Colossians 2:14, 15). The cross, then, becomes a trophy of victory where the conqueror hangs the spoils of the enemy. Yes, "it is finished!" The conflict has come to an end and our mighty Deliverer has triumphed. He has conquered both spiritual death and physical death.

Now someone may remind me that Christians as well as non-Christians still die. You are quite right in your conclusion. However, death does not end all. Satan has no claim upon our bodies after death as he did the body of Moses (Jude 9). When our Lord died on the cross and rose again He took from Satan all power over death, and now Christ only can say, "I am he that liveth, and was dead; and, behold, I am alive for evermore, Amen; and have the keys of hell and of death" (Revelation 1:18). The Victor over death ever lives and He has the complete mastery over the bodies and souls of all men. His is undisputed authority. "It is finished."

All is finished that needs to be finished to complete God's plan of salvation. Nothing can be added to the finished work of our Lord Jesus Christ. Some of you have attended church for years, depending upon your religion, ritual or the recitation of a prayer, the Ten Commandments or the Golden Rule. But none of these has ever saved your soul. You must receive the Saviour and trust His finished work for salvation. The religion of the average person is a "do" religion, but true Biblical Christianity is a "done" religion. You can do absolutely nothing to save yourself simply because Christ has already done all that God requires for your salvation. So, why not receive Christ at once! Stop trying, and trust.

Chapter 8

THE SEVENTH WORD

CHRIST'S INVINCIBILITY

Father, into thy hands I commend my spirit.
—Luke 23:46

A. A WORD OF CONQUEST

B. A WORD OF CONFIDENCE

Chapter 8

CHRIST'S INVINCIBILITY

Father, into thy hands I commend my spirit.
— Luke 23:46

LET US DRAW NEAR with reverence and respect as we listen for our Lord's last statement before His death. What will the bleeding and forsaken Son of God say? Will He turn upon His tormentors to warn them that one day they will get their due reward for what they did to Him? Not at all! They had heard Him say all that He intended to say to them. He had told them the truth and they despised Him for it. And so, dying as a criminal, and deserted by many of His friends, He turned to the Father in deepest devotion and confidence.

This final statement of the dying Saviour was a prayer. Not all of His words from the cross were prayers. Three of them, the first, fourth and seventh were addressed to the Father. It is good when a man's thoughts and words flow Godward in his dying moments, but it is unlikely that they will if prayer was not his practice in life.

I read of a man who became famous through his restaurant business. He established eating places for three thousand miles from New York to California and from Canada to the Gulf of Mexico. When at last it came time for him to die, his family gathered about his bed to hear his last words. Now please don't laugh when I tell you that they heard him whisper, "Slice the ham thin." There was nothing wrong with what he said. It means only that the ruling passion of his life showed up clearly at death. Though there may be an exception now and then, this is generally the rule.

During the past twenty-five years I have listened to a variety of expressions from dying men and women. I can tell you that a death-bed without God is a heart-rending sight. For the most part, people die much in the same way they lived. If the favor of God is to shine on our death-bed, we must know Him and fellowship with Him in life. He who dies the death of the righteous must live the life of the righteous. If it is unnatural for a man to commune with God when he is in good health and well-provided for in this life, it is not likely that he will turn to God at the hour of his death.

Jesus said, "Father." This same word introduced His first statement from the cross, "Father, forgive them; for they know not what they do." And now, "Father, into thy hands I commend my spirit." The word *Father* expresses a precious relationship. With Christ it was a relationship He always knew and enjoyed. At the age of twelve we hear Him say, "Wist ye not that I must be about my *Father's* business?" (Luke 2:49). He knew God was His Father and that He would return to His Father's house (John 14:2, 3). And now He is committing His spirit into the Father's hands knowing that soon His body will rise from the grave and ascend to the Father's house.

Notice, first, this statement is

A. *A Word of Conquest*

The mighty Victor is coming home with His trophy. His was a victorious death as well. No man had taken His life from

Him. He said as much, "Therefore doth my Father love me, because I lay down my life, that I might take it again. No man taketh it from me, but I lay it down of myself. I have power to lay it down, and I have power to take it again. This commandment have I received of my Father" (John 10:17, 18). It is true that He was "betrayed into the hands of sinners" (Matthew 26: 45), "delivered into the hands of sinful men" (Luke 24:7) and slain by "wicked hands" (Acts 2:23), but it was all voluntary on His part. It was all a part of the divine plan. He left heaven and became incarnate for this very purpose. And now that the purpose had been fulfilled, the victory was won. If in that fourth word, "My God, my God, why hast thou forsaken me?" we see the serpent bruising the heel of the woman's Seed, we see in this final word, the Seed crushing the serpent's head.

Had Christ returned to the Father's abode in heaven before accomplishing all that He came to do, He would have gone back in utter defeat. But His was a victorious death. "For this purpose the Son of God was manifested, that he might destroy the works of the devil" (I John 3:8), "that through death he might destroy him that had the power of death, that is, the devil" (Hebrews 2:14). Do not forget that Jesus went to the cross as a King, and never has this King of kings been defeated or dethroned. Above His cross were inscribed the words, "THIS IS JESUS THE KING OF THE JEWS" (Matthew 27:37). This is what He claimed for Himself and this is who He was. Death would not dare to lay its cold, clammy fingers on the holy Son of God until He Himself gave the word of permission.

Have you noticed what the Holy Spirit added to our Lord's last words? "And having said thus, he gave up the ghost" (Luke 23:46). He was not helplessly yielding to human weakness. He was not just dying. "He *gave up* the ghost," that is, He was breathing out His life voluntarily. He was not gasping for breath in an attempt to prolong life. Do not forget that "the last enemy that shall be destroyed is death" (I Corinthians 15:26), and the last Adam, who is Master over death, is the One to do it. He is the invincible Christ, and this is the "word of invincibility." The King was at that moment commanding death to convey Him to the Father's house.

Here is a comforting word for all of God's children. Ever since the cross, death, for the believer, has been but a doorway to heaven. This was not so before Calvary, but it is true now. In this connection, His second word to the penitent thief is significant: "To day shalt thou be with me in paradise" (Luke 23:43). Had that believing criminal died the day before Christ died, his spirit would have gone to a specially prepared place for the departed spirits of the dead. Instead, he went to be with Christ, and Christ went to be with the Father. Now, when the believer dies, he departs "to be with Christ" (Philippians 1:23), and he is "absent from the body to be present with the Lord" (II Corinthians 5:8). Thus the one who is truly a child of God can say "to die is gain" (Philippians 1:21). Christ's victory in His death becomes our victory in death.

Now there is a distinction between Christ's death and our death which should be noted. Unless our Lord Jesus Christ comes first, we must all die. Like Polycarp and Luther and Huss and Bunyan, we too can say, "Father, into thy hands I commend my spirit," and I believe that God will accept these words, and us, if we are saved. But we cannot utter them in the sense in which Christ spoke them. He had the power to retain life. He was not dying passively, but actively and voluntarily. Now mark well, His death was not premature; it was no suicide. It was His moment to die, and being omniscient He knew precisely when that moment was to be. It was necessary that He should die *then*, only because He took that necessity upon Himself. We cannot give up the ghost, or yield our spirit as He did, but when our time comes to die, we can be ready to give it up.

Like Paul, we should be able to say, "For I am now ready to be offered, and the time of my departure is at hand" (II Timothy 4:6). Paul had no control over the time of his death; he had been sentenced to die by a court of law. But the fact remains that he was prepared to die. And knowing that he would go at once into God's presence made death to him the hour of triumph.

Notice, next, this last statement of our Lord is

B. *A Word of Confidence*

I see in this word the certainty of confidence. And why not? Is Christ not committing all into the hands of the Father? The very essence of security and confidence in this life and in the life to come is to put our all into God's hands. The Father's hand is the place of security. Our Lord said, "My Father, which gave them me, is greater than all; and no man is able to pluck them out of my Father's hand" (John 10:29). Here is the basis of all confidence.

We dare not overlook the fact that this seventh word of our Lord was uttered prophetically centuries before His Incarnation. It is recorded in Psalm 31, and it formed a part of the evening devotions of pious Jews. It brought comfort to them before they closed their eyes in sleep. When I was a boy, some children I knew were taught to say at bedtime,

> Now I lay me down to sleep,
> I pray Thee, Lord, my soul to keep.
> And if I die before I wake,
> I pray Thee, Lord, my soul to take.

Now I see nothing wrong with this prayer, except that it might be uttered, as many prayers are, by someone who had not received the Lord Jesus Christ as Saviour. But for those who are redeemed, it is an assuring experience to know that at death, whether it be day or night, you have committed your soul to God.

The prayer recorded by David, which the Hebrews included in their evening devotions, was a prayer of restful trust and confidence in Jehovah. "Into thine hand I commit my spirit" (Psalm 31:5). There is nothing like the prayers in the Bible to bring comfort and confidence to the heart that knows God. You see, this prayer is that of a redeemed soul, for the verse goes on to say, "Thou hast redeemed me, O LORD God of truth." The redeemed soul belongs to God, therefore that is reason enough for a child of God to give himself up entirely to his Heavenly Father.

There is no language like the language of the Bible, whether in life or in death. There are many good books in the world but they are irrelevant in the hour of death. The Lord Jesus knew exactly where to go for words that suited Him when He was about to pass over. As a boy He had listened to it in the synagogue and heard it in the home. But He did not wait till death to make use of it. It was His constant practice to refer to the Scriptures. For instance, when He was being tempted of the devil, He answered him with the words, "It is written." Frequently He could be heard saying, "Have ye not read?" He relied on the Scriptures all through His lifetime, and He found them reliable even in the hour of death.

Now you surely must have noticed by now that Jesus did not quote David's text in its entirety. Two changes are worth observing. Our Lord added something at the beginning of His final statement which is not in Psalm 31:5, and He omitted something at the close. At the beginning He added the term, "Father." This word does not appear in the psalm. As a matter of fact, men did not address God as Father in Old Testament times. God is called the Father of the nation of Israel as a whole, but the term was not used in connection with individuals until after the coming of our Lord Jesus Christ. He introduced this new consciousness of God. Moreover, it is never used in reference to the entire human race. The idea of the universal father-hood of God is not taught in the Scriptures. The Father of our Lord Jesus Christ becomes our Father upon our receiving Christ as Saviour and Lord. He said, "No man cometh unto the Father but by me" (John 14:6). And how blessed it is that when we come to Christ, His Father becomes our Father! "Behold, what manner of love the Father hath bestowed upon us, that we should be called the sons of God . . ." (I John 3:1).

Then notice how Jesus at the close omitted the words, "Thou hast redeemed me, O LORD God of truth." The cry of the psalmist was that of a sinner coming to God for salvation. The cry of Christ was that of the Saviour coming to God after having provided salvation for sinners. It would have been wrong for Jesus to quote the words, "Thou hast redeemed me." He was the sinless Son of God who needed no redemption. As a matter of fact, He was, and is, the world's only Redeemer. And now that God has given His Son to die for us, we can say to Him, "Thou hast redeemed me."

This last word from the lips of the dying Saviour has a per-sonal application for each believing sinner who has trusted Him for salvation. It means that we can die as Jesus died, with the full assurance of faith and confidence that our Father in heaven will receive us. No child of God need ever fear death. Its sting is gone forever (I Corinthians 15:55), and we can say with the psalmist, "Yea, though I walk through the valley of the shadow of death, I will fear no evil: for thou art with me; thy rod and thy staff they comfort me" (Psalm 23:4). If we Christians die before Jesus comes to take His Church to heaven, we can die with the certainty of coming resurrection and immortality of our bodies. And in the meantime, between death and resurrection, our spirits will be with the Lord.

My friend, if death were to come to you now, and you were conscious in your last moments, can you say as did Stephen,

"Lord Jesus, receive my spirit" (Acts 7:59)? Do you have the certainty that you are perfectly safe in Christ? If the words of our Lord and of Stephen are yours and mine now, then we have not merely learned the art of living, but of dying as well. Frankly, I have no desire to chance a venture into eternity alone. This is why I have made a committal to Jesus Christ, and now I can say with Paul, "I know whom I have believed, and am persuaded that he is able to keep that which I have committed unto him against that day" (II Timothy 1:12).

Do not close this little book until you have said to God, "Father, into thy hands I commend my spirit." Then, whatever happens to your body in this life, you may be certain that your soul will be safe. With quiet confidence and in conquest, it is possible for you to die. As confidently as a little child lays its head on mother's breast, you can place your soul's destiny in the hands of God. This is the secret of how to live and die in peace.

It has been told that when the famous evangelist D. L. Moody lay dying, those who gathered about him heard him say, "Heaven is opening, earth is receding. Do not be alarmed; this is my coronation day." With this confidence Mr. Moody lived, and with this confidence he died. You may have this experience now by receiving the Lord Jesus Christ as your own Saviour.

Again, I must say, do not close this book until you have said to God, "Father, into thy hands I commend my spirit."

BIBLIOGRAPHY

Blackwood, Andrew W. Jr., *The Voice from the Cross* (Baker Book House, Grand Rapids), 1955.

Chappell, Clovis G., *The Seven Words* (Abingdon Press, Nashville), 1952.

Clow, William M., *The Day of the Cross* (Baker Book House, Grand Rapids), n.d.

Dixon, A. C., *The Glories of the Cross* (Eerdman's, Grand Rapids), 1962.

Ford, W. Herschel, *Seven Simple Sermons on the Saviour's Last Words* (Zondervan Publishing House, Grand Rapids), 1953.

Hobbs, Herschel H., *The Crucial Words From Calvary* (Baker Book House, Grand Rapids), n.d.

Jones, Russell Bradley, *Gold from Golgotha* (Baker Book House, Grand Rapids), 1957.

Morgan, G. Campbell, *The Westminster Pulpit, Vol. 6* (Revell, Westwood, N.J.), n.d.

Ockenga, Harold John, *Protestant Preaching in Lent* (Eerdman's, Grand Rapids), 1957.

Pink, Arthur W., *The Seven Sayings of the Saviour on the Cross* (Baker Book House, Grand Rapids), n.d.

Ricard, Olfert, *Seven Times He Spoke* (Augsburg, Minneapolis), 1960.

Seiss, J. A. and others, *Sermons and Outlines on the Seven Words* (Baker Book House, Grand Rapids), n.d.

Todd, G. Hall, *Seven Words of Love* (Baker Book House, Grand Rapids), n.d.

Turnbull, Ralph G., *The Seven Words From the Cross* (Baker Book House, Grand Rapids), 1956.

Wallis, Charles L., *Lenten-Easter Sourcebook* (Abingdon, Nashville), 1961.

SCRIPTURE INDEX

112